ADOLESCENTS, ALCOHOL
AND DRUGS

ADOLESCENTS, ALCOHOL AND DRUGS

A Practical Guide for Those Who Work With Young People

By

JUDITH H. JAYNES, M.S.W., Ph.D.

Eastlake Counseling
Milwaukee, Wisconsin

and

CHERYL A. RUGG, M.S.W., C.A.O.D.A.C.

De Paul Rehabilitation Hospital
Milwaukee, Wisconsin

CHARLES C THOMAS • PUBLISHER
Springfield • Illinois • U.S.A.

Published and Distributed Throughout the World by
CHARLES C THOMAS • PUBLISHER
2600 South First Street
Springfield, Illinois 62794-9265

© *1988 by* CHARLES C THOMAS • PUBLISHER
ISBN 0-398-05393-6
Library of Congress Catalog Card Number: 87-17978

With THOMAS BOOKS *careful attention is given to all details of manufacturing and
design. It is the Publisher's desire to present books that are satisfactory as to their physical
qualities and artistic possibilities and appropriate for their particular use.* THOMAS
BOOKS *will be true to those laws of quality that assure a good name and good will.*

Printed in the United States of America
Q-R-3

Library of Congress Cataloging in Publication Data

Jaynes, Judith H.
   Adolescents, alcohol, and drugs.

   Bibliography: p.
   Includes index.
   1. Youth—United States—Substance use. 2. Sub-
stance abuse—United States—Prevention. I. Rugg,
Cheryl A. II. Title. [DNLM: 1. Alcohol Drink-
ing—in adolescence. 2. Substance Abuse—in adoles-
cence. 3. Substance Dependence—in adolescence.
WM 270 J42a]
HV4999.Y68J39   1987   362.2'9286   87-17978
ISBN 0-398-05393-6

PREFACE

PROFESSIONALS across the nation who deal with adolescents are faced with numerous challenges. Just as our youth are faced with challenges, so are the adults who have the responsibility of guiding these young people. Our youth must make choices and decisions never before available to teens, and those who work with young people must select among numerous theories regarding how to respond to them. Drug and alcohol abuse has become a complex problem with our young people. The national data tell us that by the time adolescents leave high school, they will have had a high degree of exposure to peer alcohol and drug abuse and will themselves have a high probability of using and/or abusing alcohol and drugs. In addition, we are seeing second-generation drug abusers, adolescents whose parents themselves abused drugs as young people. Also, we are seeing a population of young people who are experiencing numerous other problems as well. They are children of alcoholics or victims of incest or child abuse. Some come from economically deprived families and others suffer from learning disabilities. Still other young people are clogging our juvenile justice system with everything from petty crimes to violent crimes against other people. Some of our youth suffer from such serious despair and depression that suicide appears to be their only answer.

A common denominator in many of these cases is drug and alcohol abuse on the part of the young people involved. In some instances, the alcohol or drug abuse is the primary problem which in turn causes the other problems. In other situations, other problems exist which highly predispose an adolescent to serious problems with drugs or alcohol while attempting to resolve those problems. It is therefore imperative for those professionals working with young people in any capacity, whether it is in school, family counseling agency, residential treatment facility, group home, or psychiatric facility, to have a thorough understanding of the dynamics of chemical dependency and the adolescent.

This book is designed to thoroughly acquaint therapists, school counselors and nurses, teachers, psychologists, psychiatrists, family therapists, social workers, recreation leaders and youth workers, and those in
the juvenile court system, with the phenomenon of adolescent chemical
dependency. The book explains not only the characteristics and dynamics of chemical abuse and dependency but also discusses the complex in-
terrelationship of chemical dependency with other adolescent problems.
This book combines research with practical interpretation to make the
latest research in the field useful to all professionals. Added to this, the
reader will find extremely useful the practical insights developed by
these authors after years of experience in working with chemically dependent adolescents and their families. This book places particular focus
on the school setting, since young people spend much of their time in
schools, and students' academic performance is increasingly being affected by drug and alcohol problems. The book deals with the relationships of the schools with other societal influences, including the family,
and discusses the implications of these relationships.

In addition to helping educators understand adolescent alcohol and
drug abuse and dependency and the process by which adolescents often
progress from experimentation through use and abuse and then dependency, this book helps educators to develop strategies for dealing, in the
school setting, with problems related to adolescent alcohol and drug use.
The book addresses the following questions: How can the primary responsibility of schools, that of educating students, be enhanced by a program which addresses adolescent alcohol and drug problems? How can
school personnel identify and assess adolescent alcohol and drug problems? How can school personnel be trained to implement programs
addressing the problem? How can schools work cooperatively with treatment programs to ensure success for young people who have been
through treatment for alcohol and drug problems? In what ways can
family members be included by schools in dealing with adolescents with
these problems?

It should be noted that this book should be useful not only to those
who deal directly with young people who have drug and alcohol problems but also to those who must refer students for help and need a context for making appropriate referrals. This context is provided by the
inclusion of assessment procedures and forms.

The book consists of seven chapters. Chapter One includes an introduction to the problem and a description of the stages of drug use.
Chapter Two deals with the role of chemical abuse during adolescent

development and how developmental needs are related to adolescent alcohol and drug problems. Chapter Three provides information on the assessment of adolescent alcohol and drug use and includes suggestions for conducting assessments with adolescents. Chapter Four addresses peer and societal influences on adolescent alcohol and drug use. Chapter Five presents plans which schools can develop and implement to address the problem of adolescent alcohol and drug use. Chapter Six includes a discussion of family factors related to adolescent problems with alcohol and drugs. The concluding chapter, Chapter Seven, discusses alcohol and drug treatment programs for adolescents, including goals and methods of treatment, characteristics of an effective adolescent counselor and evaluating the success of treatment.

As indicated in the title, the authors' goal is to provide practical information which is theoretically sound and which can be immediately applied by those who use the book. It is hoped that this book will help those who must deal with a very complicated problem, adolescent drug and alcohol abuse, in establishing a framework for understanding and addressing that problem.

J.H.J.
C.A.R.

ACKNOWLEDGMENTS

W E WOULD like to thank our husbands, Raymond Wlodkowski and Steve Christenson, for their encouragement and support of this project from start to finish.

Also, we appreciate the assistance of Michael Lavelli of Camelot Unlimited in obtaining permission for us to use the *Children of Alcoholics Screening Test* by John Jones.

In addition, we want to thank Margaret Peterson for her patience and professionalism in preparing this manuscript.

CONTENTS

ADOLESCENTS, ALCOHOL
AND DRUGS

CHAPTER ONE

THE PROBLEM WE FACE

The fact that illicit drug use overall is once again decreasing in popularity, albeit slowly, is the most encouraging part of the story. But the fact that there is an increasing use of cocaine in its most addicting form is certainly a sobering counterweight. Further, the overall levels of illicit drug use by our young people remain extremely high, both by historical standards in this country and by comparison to the industrialized world. In addition, we know that these adolescents will carry their drug habits into their twenties, as they enter the work force. Clearly, a great deal remains to be done.

(Johnson, Bachman, O'Malley, 1986)

A NEW PROBLEM, A NEW FIELD

THE STUDY of chemical dependency is a complex one, and the field of adolescent chemical dependency is still in many ways in its infancy. Those of us who work in this area continue to learn daily as we acquire more data and more information from our experiences in working with young people who abuse alcohol or drugs, or who are dependent on them.

During the 1950s the issues that are faced by today's adolescents with regard to drugs simply were not present. At that time, most of the focus was on the problem of alcoholism, and most identified alcoholics were adult men. The primary approach to addressing this problem was Alcoholics Anonymous (founded in 1935), a group still commanding respect for a solid history of success.

By the 1960s, treatment centers for alcoholics evolved and, at this time, it became evident that it was not just the chronic, older male alcoholics who needed help. The population of those seeking help for problems with alcohol began to include younger men, eventually women and professionals and, finally, adolescents.

3

Also, at this time drug use by young people began to increase. The 1960s brought the counterculture, with its radicalism and anti-establishment protest. The "hippies" of this era used marijuana and other drugs to symbolize their difference from the rest of society. Hallucinogens such as LSD were a vehicle for expanding consciousness. Drug users at this time were ill-informed, and newspapers were filled with accounts of overdoses, while emergency rooms overflowed with people on "bad trips."

During the 1970s, while young people continued to experiment with alcohol and drugs, increasing emphasis was placed on recognition of the problem and the development of treatment methods. At this time, adolescents were generally admitted to treatment programs designed for adults. Gradually, as more experience was gained, it became obvious that there were special problems uniquely related to adolescent chemical dependency. Because of this, specialized programs have been developed to facilitate recovery for young people.

Programs for adolescents must address a number of concerns. The issues of identification, diagnosis, intervention, assessment and treatment are more complicated with adolescents than they are with adults. For example, it is relatively easy to diagnose an adult as an alcoholic who has been drinking one quart of liquor everyday for the last ten years, has lost his job and family, and is in poor physical health. In contrast, it is not as easy to categorize a 15-year-old who drinks heavily four to five times a week and has quit school but does not see this as a problem, because he has a job in his dad's machine shop.

In adolescents, it is more difficult to differentiate alcohol or drug abuse from dependency. Young people may not have a long history of use, but they may have a serious problem. This raises a number of important questions. Would the 15-year-old be considered to be abusing alcohol, or would he be labeled chemically dependent? What determines this? Can this determination be based on how much or how often he drinks? Would his dropping out of school be considered a life problem, one of the criteria for a diagnosis of dependency? Who defines what a life problem is? Is it possible that an adolescent may appear to be chemically dependent during the teen years and "outgrow" what was an apparently temporary problem? What are other useful criteria for separating adolescents who abuse alcohol and drugs from those who are dependent on them? Finally, the most important, what does an effective intervention/treatment program provide in order to assist adolescents and their families? How can the program intervene to stop abusive use and to promote recovery for those who are dependent?

The material in this book addresses these issues. We do not assume to have irrefutable answers, and many of these questions are still being researched. However, we do have extensive experience in working with chemically dependent adolescents and their families. This book reflects this experience and the philosophy that has developed as a result. Frequently, we have found that our philosophy, and our resulting approach to dealing with the adolescent substance abuse problem, is supported by research. This research is documented in the discussions in the following chapters.

WHY DO KIDS USE DRUGS?

People who work with adolescents who are abusing alcohol and drugs often have a difficult time accepting one very important tenet: It feels good to use alcohol and drugs. Perhaps really accepting this means that people will have to look painfully close at their own use of chemicals. Adults often have difficulty applying what they know about themselves to what they observe in adolescents.

We frequently ask the people who participate in the training sessions that we conduct in schools and agencies to list all of the aspects of alcohol and drug use that they like. Initially, they find this a bit absurd, since these training sessions are designed to help people deal with the problems associated with alcohol and drug use. However, after some cajoling, the participants, working in small groups, usually produce lists with items such as the following:

Relaxes me
Helps me have fun
Allows socialization
Makes me sleep
Gives me happy feelings
Makes me feel powerful
Helps me to "fit in"
Makes me feel sexy
Loosens me up
Lets me say things I wouldn't say
Allows me to forget my problems

From this list we see that there are many appealing and seductive aspects to alcohol and drug use. Adolescents are drawn to the same good feelings that adults are. Therefore, when adults ask the questions, "Why do kids use drugs, anyway? Don't they realize how bad they are?" they need to remind themselves of their own reasons for using chemicals. The feelings that one achieves through such use are powerful and initially positive motivators. It is natural to want to seek those sensations. For the most part (unless there is some underlying psychological disorder), people do not do things that are harmful to themselves or cause them pain.

In attempting to understand and explain adolescent alcohol and drug use, one cannot ignore the fact that this use feels good and it is normal to want to feel good. This may seem obvious. However, this is often overlooked as people wonder about the problem. People become addicted, not so much because the drug produces a physical dependence, but because they want to achieve, again and again, those good feelings. Chemically dependent people have either never developed the ability to create good feelings for themselves (as is frequently the case with adolescents) or have chosen to use alcohol or drugs as an "easier" means to feel good (which is frequently the case with adults).

If alcohol and drugs were not appealing upon initial use, there would be no addiction problem. As mentioned, people begin using alcohol and drugs because it feels good. Addiction occurs when people are willing to sacrifice the quality of their lives in order to continue to produce that sense of feeling good. We have a society with values that encourage this, a society which places a strong emphasis on "taking care of ourselves" rather than others. This attitude promotes limited tolerance for pain or discomfort along with little ability to delay gratification. Relief can actually be only moments away, and this becomes a guiding force for many people.

A DANGEROUS ATTITUDE:
IT'S ONLY BOOZE, IT'S ONLY POT

Many adults in our society appear to be developing an attitude of complacency toward, and acceptance of, the use of alcohol and even marijuana by adolescents. Recent concern about the dangers of cocaine, and publicity about the cocaine-related deaths of prominent sports figures, have contributed to a view that makes the "softer" drugs seem like something to be less concerned about. Johnson, Bachman and O'Malley report in their 1986 survey of nearly 130 high schools that 6.2 percent of high school seniors report cocaine use within the past 30 days and that 17 percent of all seniors have tried cocaine. They further report that only 34 percent of all seniors believe there is a risk in trying cocaine. Also, while there has been a slight overall decline in the use of illicit drugs by adolescents, the use of cocaine has shown no appreciable change during the past year.

In light of this, many people choose to believe that alcohol and drug use is relatively harmless. This is a dangerous attitude. Alarm about the increase in the use of cocaine is not an excuse for complacency about the use of other mind-altering substances. They, too, are causing serious problems for young people and these problems cannot be ignored.

Although the 1986 survey revealed that the gradual decline in overall illicit drug use by high school students, which began four years ago, still continues, it is misleading to gain much reassurance from this. In spite of this decline, well over half of all high school seniors still report having had some experience with illicit drugs. Also, seniors still continue to report a high level of alcohol use, with 85 percent reporting use in the last year, nearly two-thirds reporting use in the past month, 37 percent admitting to having five or more drinks in a row at least once in the prior two weeks, and 5 percent reporting daily, or nearly daily, use of alcohol in the prior month.

An attitude of complacency about this situation raises great concern. Frequently, adults interpret data showing that large numbers of adolescents are drinking or are using drugs on a regular basis to mean that this is a "normal" stage and that the young people will grow out of it. This can be a dangerous interpretation. While it may appear that alcohol and drug use during the teen years is something that we can expect, that does not mean that we have to accept this behavior.

From birth through maturity, certain behaviors are expected as children move through the stages of development. Some of these behaviors are viewed as maladaptive and dangerous. While we expect these behaviors and even watch for them, parents, child-care professionals and teachers are prepared with a response to assist the child in setting boundaries and developing appropriate skills and coping mechanisms.

The behaviors of young people need responses, a kind of "mirror" for our youth. As their behavior is reflected back to them along with values about that behavior, they begin to form their own values.

Chemical use by young people is not simply a stage of growing up that adults can sit idly by and watch. Adults who do not respond when they know that adolescents are using alcohol or drugs, but rather hope

Table I

TRENDS IN ANNUAL PREVALENCE OF SIXTEEN TYPES OF DRUGS

						Percent who used in last twelve months							
Approx. N. =	Class of 1975 (9400)	Class of 1976 (15400)	Class of 1977 (17100)	Class of 1978 (17800)	Class of 1979 (15500)	Class of 1980 (15900)	Class of 1981 (17500)	Class of 1982 (17700)	Class of 1983 (16300)	Class of 1984 (15900)	Class of 1985 (16000)	Class of 1986 (15200)	'85-'86 change
Marijuana/Hashish	40.0	44.5	47.6	50.2	50.8	48.8	46.1	44.3	42.3	40.0	40.6	38.8	−1.8
Inhalants[a]	NA	3.0	3.7	4.1	5.4	4.6	4.1	4.5	4.3	5.1	5.7	6.1	+0.4
Inhalants Adjusted[b]	NA	NA	NA	NA	8.9	7.9	6.1	6.6	6.2	7.2	7.5	8.9	+1.4s
Amyl & Butyl Nitrites[c]	NA	NA	NA	NA	6.5	5.7	3.7	3.6	3.6	4.0	4.0	4.7	+0.7
Hallucinogens	11.2	9.4	8.8	9.6	9.9	9.3	9.0	8.1	7.3	6.5	6.3	6.0	−0.3
Hallucinogens Adjusted[d]	NA	NA	NA	NA	11.8	10.4	10.1	9.0	8.3	7.3	7.6	7.6	0.0
LSD	7.2	6.4	5.5	6.3	6.6	6.5	6.5	6.1	5.4	4.7	4.4	4.5	+0.1
PCP[c]	NA	NA	NA	NA	7.0	4.4	3.2	2.2	2.6	2.3	2.9	2.4	−0.5
Cocaine	5.6	6.0	7.2	9.0	12.0	12.3	12.4	11.5	11.4	11.6	13.1	12.7	−0.4
Heroin	1.0	0.8	0.8	0.8	0.5	0.5	0.5	0.6	0.6	0.5	0.6	0.5	−0.1
Other opiates[c]	5.7	5.7	6.4	6.0	6.2	6.3	5.9	5.3	5.1	5.2	5.9	5.2	−0.7s
Stimulants[c]	16.2	15.8	16.3	17.1	18.3	20.8	26.0	26.1	24.6	NA	NA	NA	NA
Stimulants Adjusted[e,f]	NA	NA	NA	NA	NA	NA	NA	20.3	17.9	17.7	15.8	13.4	−2.4sss
Sedatives[c]	11.7	10.7	10.8	9.9	9.9	10.3	10.5	9.1	7.9	6.6	5.8	5.2	−0.6
Barbiturates[c]	10.7	9.6	9.3	8.1	7.5	6.8	6.6	5.5	5.2	4.9	4.6	4.2	−0.4
Methaqualone[c]	5.1	4.7	5.2	4.9	5.9	7.2	7.6	6.8	5.4	3.8	2.8	2.1	−0.7s
Tranquilizers[c]	10.6	10.3	10.8	9.9	9.6	8.7	8.0	7.0	6.9	6.1	6.1	5.8	−0.3
Alcohol	84.8	85.7	87.0	87.7	88.1	87.9	87.0	86.8	87.3	86.0	85.6	84.5	−1.1
Cigarettes	NA	NA	NA	NA	NA	NA	NA	NA	NA	NA	NA	NA	NA

NOTES: Level of significance of difference between the two most recent classes: s = .05, ss = .01, sss = .001. NA indicates data not available.
[a]Data based on four questionnaire forms. N is four-fifths of N indicated.
[b]Adjusted for underreporting of amyl and butyl nitrites. See text for details.
[c]Data based on a single questionnaire form. N is one-fifth of N indicated.
[d]Adjusted for underreporting of PCP. See text for details.
[e]Only drug use which was not under a doctor's orders is included here.
[f]Adjusted for the inappropriate reporting of non-prescription stimulants.

SOURCE: Johnson, L.D., Bachman, J.G., and O'Malley, P.M. (February 20, 1987). Twelfth annual survey by the University of Michigan Institute for

Table II

TRENDS IN THIRTY-DAY PREVALENCE OF SIXTEEN TYPES OF DRUGS

Percent who used in last thirty days

	Class of 1975	Class of 1976	Class of 1977	Class of 1978	Class of 1979	Class of 1980	Class of 1981	Class of 1982	Class of 1983	Class of 1984	Class of 1985	Class of 1986	'85-'86 change
Approx. N =	(9400)	(15400)	(17100)	(17800)	(15500)	(15900)	(17500)	(17700)	(16300)	(15900)	(16000)	(15200)	
Marijuana/Hashish	27.1	32.2	35.4	37.1	36.5	33.7	31.6	28.5	27.0	25.2	25.7	23.4	-2.3s
Inhalants[a]	NA	0.9	1.3	1.5	1.7	1.4	1.5	1.5	1.7	1.9	2.2	2.5	+0.3
Inhalants Adjusted[b]	NA	NA	NA	NA	3.2	2.7	2.5	2.5	2.5	2.6	3.0	3.2	+0.2
Amyl & Butyl Nitrites[c]	NA	NA	NA	NA	2.4	1.8	1.4	1.1	1.4	1.4	1.6	1.3	-0.3
Hallucinogens	4.7	3.4	4.1	3.9	4.0	3.7	3.7	3.4	2.8	2.6	2.5	2.5	0.0
Hallucinogens Adjusted[d]	NA	NA	NA	NA	5.3	4.4	4.5	4.1	3.5	3.2	3.8	3.5	-0.3
LSD	2.3	1.9	2.1	2.1	2.4	2.3	2.5	2.4	1.9	1.5	1.6	1.7	+0.1
PCP[c]	NA	NA	NA	NA	2.4	1.4	1.4	1.0	1.3	1.0	1.6	1.3	-0.3
Cocaine	1.9	2.0	2.9	3.9	5.7	5.2	5.8	5.0	4.9	5.8	6.7	6.2	-0.5
Heroin	0.4	0.2	0.3	0.3	0.2	0.2	0.2	0.2	0.2	0.3	0.3	0.2	-0.1
Other opiates[e]	2.1	2.0	2.8	2.1	2.4	2.4	2.1	1.8	1.8	1.8	2.3	2.0	-0.3
Stimulants[e]	8.5	7.7	8.8	8.7	9.9	12.1	15.8	13.7	12.4	NA	NA	NA	NA
Stimulants Adjusted[e,f]	NA	NA	NA	NA	NA	NA	NA	10.7	8.9	8.3	6.8	5.5	-1.3ss
Sedatives[e]	5.4	4.5	5.1	4.2	4.4	4.8	4.6	3.4	3.0	2.3	2.4	2.2	-0.2
Barbiturates[e]	4.7	3.9	4.3	3.2	3.2	2.9	2.6	2.0	2.1	1.7	2.0	1.8	-0.2
Methaqualone[e]	2.1	1.6	2.3	1.9	2.3	3.3	3.1	2.4	1.8	1.1	1.0	0.8	-0.2
Tranquilizers[e]	4.1	4.0	4.6	3.4	3.7	3.1	2.7	2.4	2.5	2.1	2.1	2.1	0.0
Alcohol	68.2	68.3	71.2	72.1	71.8	72.0	70.7	69.7	69.4	67.2	65.9	65.3	-0.6
Cigarettes	36.7	38.8	38.4	36.7	34.4	30.5	29.4	30.0	30.3	29.3	30.1	29.6	-0.5

NOTES: Level of significance of difference between the two most recent classes: s = .05, ss = .01, sss = .001. NA indicates data not available.
[a]Data based on four questionnaire forms. N is four-fifths of N indicated.
[b]Adjusted for underreporting of amyl and butyl nitrites. See text for details.
[c]Data based on a single questionnaire form. N is one-fifth of N indicated.
[d]Adjusted for underreporting of PCP. See text for details.
[e]Only drug use which was not under a doctor's orders is included here.
[f]Adjusted for the inappropriate reporting of non-prescription stimulants.

SOURCE: Johnson, L.D., Bachman, J.G., and O'Malley, P.M. (February 20, 1987). Twelfth annual survey by the University of Michigan Institute for Social Research. *The University of Michigan News and Information Services News Release.*

Table III

TRENDS IN LIFETIME PREVALENCE OF SIXTEEN TYPES OF DRUGS

	Percent ever used												
	Class of 1975	Class of 1976	Class of 1977	Class of 1978	Class of 1979	Class of 1980	Class of 1981	Class of 1982	Class of 1983	Class of 1984	Class of 1985	Class of 1986	'85-'86 change
Approx. N. =	(9400)	(15400)	(17100)	(17800)	(15500)	(15900)	(17500)	(17700)	(16300)	(15900)	(16000)	(15200)	
Marijuana/Hashish	47.3	52.8	56.4	59.2	60.4	60.3	59.5	58.7	57.0	54.9	54.2	50.9	-3.3ss
Inhalants[a]	NA	10.3	11.1	12.0	12.7	11.9	12.3	12.8	13.6	14.4	15.4	15.9	+0.5
Inhalants Adjusted[b]	NA	NA	NA	NA	18.2	17.3	17.2	17.7	18.2	18.0	18.1	20.1	+2.0s
Amyl & Butyl Nitrites[c]	NA	NA	NA	NA	11.1	11.1	10.1	9.8	8.4	8.1	7.9	8.6	+0.7
Hallucinogens	16.3	15.1	13.9	14.3	14.1	13.3	13.3	12.5	11.9	10.7	10.3	9.7	-0.6
Hallucinogens Adjusted[d]	NA	NA	NA	NA	17.7	15.6	15.3	14.3	13.6	12.3	12.1	11.9	-0.2
LSD	11.3	11.0	9.8	9.7	9.5	9.3	9.8	9.6	8.9	8.0	7.5	7.2	-0.3
PCP[c]	NA	NA	NA	NA	12.8	9.6	7.8	6.0	5.6	5.0	4.9	4.8	-0.1
Cocaine	9.0	9.7	10.8	12.9	15.4	15.7	16.5	16.0	16.2	16.1	17.3	16.9	-0.4
Heroin	2.2	1.8	1.8	1.6	1.1	1.1	1.1	1.2	1.2	1.3	1.2	1.1	-0.1
Other opiates[e]	9.0	9.6	10.3	9.9	10.1	9.8	10.1	9.6	9.4	9.7	10.2	9.0	-1.2s
Stimulants[c]	22.3	22.6	23.0	22.9	24.2	26.4	32.2	35.6	35.4	NA	NA	NA	NA
Stimulants Adjusted[e,f]	NA	NA	NA	NA	NA	NA	NA	27.9	26.9	27.9	26.2	23.4	-2.8ss
Sedatives[c]	18.2	17.7	17.4	16.0	14.6	14.9	16.0	15.2	14.4	13.3	11.8	10.4	-1.4s
Barbiturates[c]	16.9	16.2	15.6	13.7	11.8	11.0	11.3	10.3	9.9	9.9	9.2	8.4	-0.8
Methaqualone[c]	8.1	7.8	8.5	7.9	8.3	9.5	10.6	10.7	10.1	8.3	6.7	5.2	-1.5ss
Tranquilizers[c]	17.0	16.8	18.0	17.0	16.3	15.2	14.7	14.0	13.3	12.4	11.9	10.9	-1.0
Alcohol	90.4	91.9	92.5	93.1	93.0	93.2	92.6	92.8	92.6	92.6	92.2	91.3	-0.9
Cigarettes	73.6	75.4	75.7	75.3	74.0	71.0	71.0	70.1	70.6	69.7	68.8	67.6	-1.2

NOTES: Level of significance of difference between the two most recent classes: s = .05, ss = .01, sss = .001. NA indicates data not available.
[a] Data based on four questionnaire forms. N is four-fifths of N indicated.
[b] Adjusted for underreporting of amyl and butyl nitrites. See text for details.
[c] Data based on a single questionnaire form. N is one-fifth of N indicated.
[d] Adjusted for underreporting of PCP. See text for details.
[e] Only drug use which was not under a doctor's orders is included here.
[f] Adjusted for the inappropriate reporting of non-prescription stimulants.

SOURCE: Johnson, L.D., Bachman, J.G., and O'Malley, P.M. (February 20, 1987). Twelfth annual survey by the University of Michigan Institute for *Michigan News and Information Services News Release.*

that these young people will experiment and then decide on their own not to continue the use (or to continue the use in a responsible manner), have unrealistic expectations. First, this expectation attributes greater abilities to responsibly moderate their behavior than most adolescents are developmentally capable of. Second, it ignores the powerfully addicting potential of alcohol and drugs as a way to quickly and reliably feel good.

When our children are infants, we know that they are prone to stick all kinds of things in their mouths. We don't sit still and wait for this stage to pass, because we recognize that idle experimentation with small objects could result in choking or even poisoning. We respond in two ways. We set up as many protective measures as possible so the infant is not exposed to danger. We remove objects from their reach, we choose toys without small parts, and so on. And second, we show the children that this behavior is not acceptable. We give stern commands and take small objects away while directing the child's attention elsewhere.

Why aren't we doing the same for our young people when it comes to alcohol and other drugs?

The process seems simple, but we have not transferred the basics to what we know about adolescents. Sometimes, we find ourselves doing the opposite of what good judgment tells us to do. We must ask ourselves whether we've become too intimidated by our teens demanding the right to make their own decisions and their own mistakes. Are we giving them the right to make decisions that they are not yet developmentally able to make, thereby putting them in potentially dangerous, even lethal, situations? We would not watch a one-year-old swallow a penny; we must not watch our teenagers drink or use drugs.

Enabling

When adolescents do develop problems from the use of alcohol or drugs, often parents who have not taken a firm stand on the issue feel guilty. They then try to take steps that protect their child from dealing with the consequences of their alcohol and drug use because they, themselves, feel responsible. This compounds the problem and often makes the situation worse, because the problem is not then directly addressed.

Protecting one's child is normal and appropriate, but overprotection can cause problems. Enablers overprotect. They find it difficult to separate what their child needs from what their child wants. The price of overprotection is prolonging the dependency of immaturity and thereby aiding the progress of chemical dependency.

(Macdonald, 1984, p. 38)

Enabling is destructive, because it does not allow the young person to face the consequences of his or her behavior or to take responsibility for that behavior. Though not intended to do so, enabling supports the problem behavior and, in many ways, encourages it to continue.

If adults continue to believe "it's only booze or pot," we will see in the next generation a large number of chemically dependent individuals with major life problems, and *we* will have enabled it. We must change the attitude of complacency and acceptance of substance abuse to give our youth the fair chance they deserve.

THE ISSUE OF ABSTINENCE

There are a variety of reasons why individuals choose to abstain from the use of alcohol or drugs. Many people choose not to use alcohol or drugs based on religious beliefs and, of course, some religions forbid the use of any mood-altering substances at all. Also, there are some people who believe that it is unhealthy and physically harmful to use alcohol or drugs and they choose to abstain for these reasons.

A large number of people who have grown up in homes that were disrupted by the use of alcohol or drugs have made the decision to abstain in reaction to the dysfunction they experienced in their families. For these people, alcohol or drugs may have very negative associations. Because of this, they often find it difficult to relate to situations where people drink or use drugs to enhance enjoyment.

Most recovering alcoholics and drug addicts remain abstinent, or work toward abstinence, as part of their recovery program. This is true because they have made a decision that this is most beneficial to them. This decision is also supported by the principles of Alcoholics Anonymous.

There is, however, some controversy in the field of alcohol treatment about whether abstinence is a necessary goal. There are some who argue that a goal of controlled drinking may be more realistic, and this view has created heated conflict among those in the field (Peele, 1984).

It is our stand that abstinence is an important and necessary goal in treatment programs for adolescents. One primary reason for this is the developmental vulnerability of young people. (This is discussed in more detail in Chapter Two.) The rapidity with which many adolescents progress through the stages of drug use, and the destruction that such progression causes, creates a strong argument for the advocacy of abstinence.

Also, there is evidence that there are certain ages when adolescents are most at risk for initiation into the use of drugs. If there is no use of alcohol or drugs during that time, there is much less likelihood that later problems will develop. For example, Kandel and Logan (1984) report that the age for initiation into the use of marijuana begins at age 13, rises to a peak at age 18, with a sharp drop between age 19 and 20. The risk to initiate marijuana use after age 20 is quite small. Simply put, if they haven't tried it by age 20, chances are they won't. (For alcohol, the age range for initiation is age 10 through 18, with a peak at age 14.)

Kandel and Logan also found that periods of highest use for marijuana and alcohol decline sharply after age 20 as well. They suggest that both the decline in risk of initiation and the decline in level of use can be attributed to the maturational process and movement into adulthood. In essence, the roles of adulthood are incompatible with continued use.

The findings of their study show that there are some adolescents who use alcohol and/or drugs quite heavily, yet move into adulthood possessing the skills necessary to assume adult responsibilities and to function as productive adults. However, data are still scarce that would allow us to accurately predict which adolescents might move through periods of heavy alcohol or drug use and remain unaffected, and which may suffer serious life consequences. Developmentally, adolescence is a time when people are highly vulnerable to the development of problems and dependencies. Because of this, for those who live and work with young people who are struggling with these issues, a focus on advocating for a substance-free adolescence makes sense.

Additionally, it is illegal for adolescents to use both alcohol and drugs. Those who work with young people know that the demonstration of responsible behavior is a sign of growing maturity. Indulging in illegal behavior is not generally considered to be responsible. Therefore, a stand advocating abstinence is a critical part of an effective adolescent treatment program.

STAGES OF DRUG USE

Adolescents do not begin using alcohol and drugs with the intention of becoming dependent on them. In fact, they begin their use with very little understanding of the inherent dangers of alcohol and drug use, and virtually no willingness to accept the possibility that such dangers might even exist. Developmentally, adolescents are at a stage where they view themselves as generally invulnerable. They operate under the assumption that "it can never happen to me," and they genuinely believe that dangerous or life-threatening events will not happen to them. Therefore, when their drug use has progressed to a stage where associated problems have begun to emerge, they often are not able to recognize the seriousness of the situation.

In understanding the stages of the progression of alcohol and drug use which moves from experimentation through dependence, it is important to emphasize that all adolescents who experiment with alcohol and drugs do not automatically move on to the next stage and then to the next. Some adolescents experiment and stop there. Others make a decision (which is sometimes an unconscious one) to move on to social use and go no further than this. Still others continue on through misuse, abuse and dependence.

There are a number of factors that influence whether or not an adolescent's alcohol or drug use progresses through these stages, and they are discussed in more detail in subsequent chapters. The important point here is that while experimentation with alcohol or drugs does not necessarily predict later problems, it is a first step in the progression. Therefore, interventions aimed at stopping adolescent alcohol and drug use as early as possible are suggested as preventative measures.

The stages of the alcohol and drug use progression are essentially the same for adults and adolescents (see Table IV). However, adolescents often move through the progression more quickly. They are at a developmentally vulnerable point, and the effects that they have learned they can achieve through the use of alcohol or drugs provide powerful motivators. Simply put, from the perspective of the adolescent, "This makes me feel good. I don't know how to get this feeling any other way. I want it again. So I'll get high again."

Stage One: Experimentation— Learning the Mood Swing

The initial stage of drug use involves learning the basic effects of alcohol or drugs. Through casual and infrequent experimentation, adolescents learn that the use of alcohol or drugs produces a change in mood and this change is usually in a highly positive direction. They learn that this change is reliable. They find that each time they use a certain drug, they can produce the same predictable sensation. This is very powerful for adolescents who experience very little personal consistency with frequent fluctuations, both emotionally and physically, as they continue to mature. They also learn that they can count on the effects and that they can control them through controlling the amount of alcohol or drugs used over a specific period of time.

At the stage of experimentation, adolescents are learning "what happens to me if I use alcohol or drugs." These are the basics that all individuals learn in the early stages of experimentation. During this stage there is little obvious behavior change and usually no noticeable problems. At this stage, tolerance is low and small amounts of use can produce euphoria with a return to a normal state afterwards.

Adolescents do not often stay in the experimentation stage for an indefinite period of time. Some may make a decision not to use alcohol or drugs any more. This decision may be made for any number of reasons, including satisfaction of curiosity, fear of being caught, and health and safety concerns. Others may find the euphoric effects so compelling and the relief of stress so profound after they use alcohol or drugs, that they then move to the next stage, that of social use.

Stage Two: Social Use— Application of What is Learned to Social Situations

During the stage of social use, adolescents are in control of how much they use, when they use and the effects of their use. At this stage, alcohol or drugs are being used in moderation and for a clearly defined and beneficial purpose. Essentially, during this stage, adolescents demonstrate a great deal of responsibility in their alcohol or drug use. They have learned through experimentation how much of a substance is needed to produce what type of effect, and they can regulate their use based on this information.

At this time, certain "rules" are developed which dictate when alcohol or drug use is permissible and when it is not. The outcome is then planned and predictable. These rules involve such limitations as "no use during the school day," "no use at school activities," "no drinking and driving," and "no purchasing of substances." At this stage, adolescents can, and do, set appropriate controls on their alcohol or drug use.

However, frequency of alcohol or drug use during this stage is likely to increase (though usually still limited to weekend use), and this creates a situation of high risk for progression toward the more advanced stages

TABLE IV

STAGES OF ALCOHOL AND DRUG USE PROGRESSION

	Experimentation: Learning the Mood Swing	Social Use: Application to Social Situations	Misuse: Seeking the Mood Swing	Abuse: Preoccupation with the Mood Swing	Chemical Dependency: Using to Feel Normal
Frequency	Occasional use; 1-2 x monthly. "Behind the barn" kind of using.	Moderation; 2-3 x monthly, usually weekends. Rules developed to regulate use.	Regular, weekly use, 1-2 x per week. Use during the day may begin.	3-4 x per week.	Daily use; all day
Tolerance	No tolerance. Small amount produces intoxication. 1-2 beers.	Tolerance begins. 2-4 beers.	Tolerance increases. 4-6 beers.	High tolerance. 6-10 beers. Possible blackouts.	Extreme tolerance. Decreased tolerance possible. Blackouts probable.
Control	Outcome planned and predictable. Intoxication rare and due to inexperience.		Intoxications begin to occur with regularity.	Intoxications continue. Usage unpredictable. Can't be sure when or how much. Plans and promises made to self and others to cut down or quit, sometimes followed by brief respite with a subsequent return to using.	Usage totally out of control. No predictability. Negative consequences occur one after the other.
Mood Alteration	Euphoria with a return to a normal state after using.	Euphoria continues. Adolescent interprets the high as pleasurable.	Euphoria continues. Increased tolerance produces hangovers.	Non-using produces a letdown and depression. Euphoria is elusive.	Adolescent no longer able to function physically and mentally without using. Severe letdown without using. Using returns adolescent to a state that feels normal.

TABLE IV (Continued)

Feelings	Excitement, fun, fear of getting caught. Thrill of acting grown up and independent. Feels a sense of belonging.	Beginnings of guilt, fear, shame. Pride in being able to drink more than other adolescents.		Depression. Anger. Loneliness. Potential for suicidal thoughts or attempts.	Severe depression, alienation. Suicidal thoughts or actions.
Goal	Experimentation.	Socialization.	Getting high. Avoidance of pain or discomfort. Relief from adolescent inadequacy.	Staying high.	Avoidance of depression or letdown.
Sources	Friends. Family liquor cabinet.	Friends. Siblings. Begin buying small quantities to use in one evening.	Buying large enough quantities to always be prepared.	Selling drugs. Selling allows the seller to keep a supply after sale for themselves. May begin stealing such as from school lockers and teacher's desks.	Any way possible. Tremendous risks taken to get high. Usually associated with crime—shoplifting, burglaries.
What the World Sees	Little change.	Parents begin grounding; question why things are changing. Subtle attitude change. May get caught in school high or using. Decrease in productive leisure time activities. Decline in school performance—recent. Mood swings. Mixture of using and non-using friends. Lying, conning behavior. Friends not introduced to parents.		Parents know things are out of control but are confused. Groundings increase. Defensive, angry attitude. Stealing. Poor school attendance. Obvious personality change. Few non-using friends. Elaborate schemes to cover use.	Parents feel as if they have lost their child—as if they no longer know him/her. Physical deterioration; unhealthy, disheveled looking. Loss of weight. Poor memory. No non-using friends. School dropout, expulsion. Lies erode or are poorly constructed. Lack of concern about being caught. Runs away from home.

of abuse and dependence. The inexperience and immaturity of adolescents frequently keep them from recognizing that they may have moved to a deeper level of involvement with alcohol or drugs.

Stage Three: Misuse — Seeking the Mood Swing

During this stage, the focus of the use of alcohol or drugs is no longer specifically on socializing. At this stage, adolescents are more interested in using alcohol or drugs because they want to get high. Achieving the euphoric effect has become more important than having a good time with their friends.

Another shift takes place during this stage. We begin to see using alcohol or drugs to the point of intoxication occurring more frequently. These adolescents may not be experiencing any problems in their lives, but the potential for problems is always there because of the intoxication.

While alcohol and drug use is not yet out of control at this point, with the motivator for use changed from socialization to getting high, there is an increase in frequency of use. Using alcohol or drugs may occur not just on weekends but from two to four times per week at this time.

At this stage, adolescents experience a great deal of excitement and anticipation about their alcohol and drug use along with occasional feelings of guilt and fear after becoming intoxicated. The peer group of adolescents at this stage usually consists of both friends who use alcohol and drugs and those who do not. Overall, these adolescents experience intense ambivalence about the situation but are, in many ways, preparing to move on to a more advanced stage of abuse.

Erratic school performance becomes apparent often with declining grades, behavior problems or attitudinal changes. It is common for parents to respond to this turn of events with: "This is just a stage. All kids try alcohol or drugs, at least a little. How else will they learn how to handle it?" At the same time, the adolescent frequently rationalizes: "It's no big deal. I can handle it. All the kids do it."

These attitudes can be dangerous. Due to the relative inexperience of adolescents, getting high is not as harmless as it may appear. There are potential results which are much more serious than a simple hangover, and these are seen frequently by those who work in adolescent treatment programs. The following case example illustrates the point.

Todd was arrested for drunk driving and manslaughter by reckless use of an automobile. He was the cause of an accident that occurred while he was drunk. This accident resulted in the death of a 17-year-old girl. Todd, age 17, was shy and somewhat withdrawn, but psychological testing revealed that this was within normal ranges for an adolescent of his age. He drank before a school dance so that he could be relaxed enough to approach a girl he was interested in. He drank after the dance, because his efforts were not successful and he was feeling upset. During his drive home the accident occurred. Todd entered a treatment program on the advice of his attorney, who felt it would strengthen his case in court. All evidence of assessments indicated that he was not chemically dependent but certainly that he was at risk for more serious problems due to his behavior toward alcohol (seeking a high) and the relief he obtained from feeling the normal adolescent sense of inadequacy. Todd was waived to adult court and convicted of involuntary manslaughter. He spent one year in prison followed by three years of probation. Todd carries a permanent felony conviction in spite of his good academic standing, regular church attendance, strong value system and an extremely caring, nurturing family. In this case, relative inexperience during the seeking stage led to problems that Todd could never have anticipated.

Stage Four: Abuse — Preoccupation With the Mood Swing

During the abuse stage, we see a shift from simply seeking the mood swing to a preoccupation with being high. It is during this stage that problems begin to build up and become more obvious to those people involved in the life of the adolescent. For both the abusing adolescent as well as affected family members, there is a sense that as soon as one problem is solved another emerges. Parents at this time often express the feeling that as soon as they have put one fire out, another has started.

The adolescent's peer group, by this time, consists primarily of other young people who are also abusing drugs. This can happen in two ways. The peer group may have shifted to the same level of use, or adolescents at this stage may have found a peer group with a level of alcohol or drug use consistent with their own use. The peer group at this time is one with whom they feel safe from criticism.

Frequency of use during this stage increases, often to the point of daily use. "Rules" which dictate use no longer limit when not to use alcohol or drugs but, rather, focus on when such use can occur. "Only parties where drinking and drug use are permitted are worth going to." "Smoking a joint before school is something I have to do." "I would never go out with her. She's straight." "I have to snort coke during my lunch hour."

During this stage stealing often occurs. This may include shoplifting or pilfering money from parents' wallets or purses. Also involvement with the police for such things as disorderly conduct, possession, or burglaries may begin to increase in frequency. At this time, many adolescents begin developing elaborate systems of lies to cover their actions. In addition, truancy and school failure are common, and if the adolescent at this stage has a job, chances are it will be lost.

Adolescents frequently experience periods of depression accompanied by guilt during this stage and parents begin to question what is going on. Parents know things have changed and they wonder if all adolescents experience so many problems. They may seek the help of a school counselor or confer with police officers specializing in youth work. Some may turn to psychiatrists or other mental health professionals for help. If these people are knowledgeable about adolescent chemical abuse, they can help parents accept that their child may have a serious problem with alcohol or drugs. If not, parents may continue to search for answers until they finally find someone who identifies the problem. And, sometimes, the adolescent must move to the final stage of dependency before help is eventually found.

Stage Five: Chemical Dependency —
Using Alcohol or Drugs to Feel Normal

At this stage, alcohol or drug use is no longer fun for the chemically dependent adolescent. The use simply forestalls the bad feelings that occur when the adolescent is not high or under the influence. The dependent adolescent uses alcohol or drugs because it is a way of life, not because it is fun. The use of alcohol or drugs no longer creates the euphoria it once did. Instead, it is necessary to maintain a sense of normalcy for the adolescent.

Discussions among chemically dependent adolescents about their alcohol and drug use are dramatically different than discussions among adolescents who are in the early stages of alcohol and drug use. Nondependent adolescents talk about the good times, laughter and fun, the excitement, the euphoria. In contrast, dependent young people discuss their alcohol or drug use as a given, or a matter of fact. They use these substances because they must.

For dependent adolescents, their use of alcohol or drugs is completely out of control. Most of the time, their frequency of use has progressed to regular daily use. These young people are unable to control how much or how often they use alcohol or drugs. At the same time, they tell those around them that they are in full control and can decide to quit at any time. Tolerance is at a high level, and they are consuming more alcohol or drugs than ever as they seek the euphoria that has been lost to chemical dependency.

Young people at this stage have increased their ability to consume toxic amounts of alcohol or drugs, and, as a result, the risk of an overdose with physical complications (or death) is high. This is especially true if they are mixing alcohol and/or other drugs. Chemically dependent adolescents are no longer able to determine or predict the outcome of their alcohol or drug use. They find themselves involved in burglaries, disorderly conduct, truancy, and stealing from family members.

Dependent adolescents make well-intended promises in an attempt to prove that they are still in control. They promise not to miss more school, they promise to repay stolen money, they promise not to have parties when their parents are not home. But intentions are meaningless in the life of the chemically dependent adolescent. These young people have one goal, and that is to avoid feeling bad. At this point, this can only be achieved through the use of alcohol or drugs. They know of no other options for dealing with negative feelings, and when they feel guilty and depressed about their alcohol or drug use, they get high to deal with this. Thus, they create and recreate the vicious cycle of dependency.

Adolescents at this stage are often referred to treatment programs. This referral may be made by school counselors, parents, members of the clergy or representatives of the juvenile court system. (Frequently, by this time, these young people have experienced legal difficulties.)

When chemically dependent adolescents are referred for treatment, they usually have no awareness of the connection between the many problems that they have been having in their lives and the fact that they are using alcohol and drugs. They often find it shocking to hear that they will be expected to remain abstinent during their treatment program and afterwards. They may even agree to the goal of abstinence with a hidden agenda of, "I'll show them I can use drugs and still get my life in order." They usually know that there is trouble in their lives. However, they enter treatment programs, not wanting to stop the use of chemicals, but wanting to relieve the pressure they are receiving from parents, schools or the courts.

Families of chemically dependent adolescents are usually experiencing tremendous chaos. Parents often feel ashamed, because they believe they should have been able to handle a problem which has now become completely out of control. It is common for parents to blame each other, and this creates even more tension due to the marital discord. Siblings frequently feel ignored and uncared for, as all of the energy in the family is focused on the dependent young person. As a result, they themselves may turn to the use of alcohol or drugs. For these reasons, all members of the family will need to be included in the treatment program.

By the time these young people reach treatment programs, they are often depressed, angry and withdrawn. Many are, or have been, suicidal and almost all have serious problems at school if they have not already dropped out. Even though they recognize that there are problems, they usually resent being in a treatment program. Chemically dependent adolescents rarely refer themselves for treatment.

People who work with adolescents frequently want an answer. They want to know, "Are they or are they not chemically dependent?" As previously discussed, the answer is not as important as is the determination of both how seriously affected the adolescent's life is as well as the type of intervention or treatment which is required. It is particularly easy to confuse the stages of abuse and chemical dependency. This confusion highlights the diagnostic difficulties most professionals experience when assessing an adolescent. Adolescents can move through the progression of the stages so quickly that they take on features of chemical dependency. Yet, the impact of a major event or intervention can reduce or stop using, and it then becomes clear that the diagnosis should be abuse. Unfortunately, it is difficult to differentiate the abusing adolescent from the chemically dependent adolescent in advance. This differentiation often occurs after the fact. For this reason treatment implications for these two stages are virtually the same (see Chapter 7).

Adolescent chemical dependency is a complex issue and can be looked at from a number of perspectives. The next chapter examines the developmental factors in adolescence that contribute to problems with alcohol and drugs.

CHAPTER TWO

THE ROLE OF CHEMICAL ABUSE DURING ADOLESCENT DEVELOPMENT

The adolescent moves from day to day, situation to situation — like an open wound, painful, tender to touch — vulnerable, in need of appropriate coping mechanisms, newer ways to resolve various bewildering stresses, and validation from the many arenas of his life. For some the "high" gained from chemicals begins to provide an answer. Euphoric substances help the adolescent to cope, medicate his stresses rather quickly, and provide him with status and a feeling of belonging in a using peer group and culture.

(Huberty and Malmquist, 1978)

ADOLESCENT alcohol and drug abuse often confuses and puzzles adults. It is hard for many adults to understand why people who appear to have almost limitless possibilities ahead of them, not to mention what appears to be the freedom of being young and without responsibilities, seem to irrationally ruin their lives because of problems with the use of alcohol or drugs.

One reason for this lack of understanding is that adults frequently tend to romanticize their own adolescence, forgetting what a painful and conflictual time this can be. Another related explanation is that adults often lack an awareness of the pressing human needs which dominate during adolescence and of the use that chemicals play in meeting those needs for many adolescents.

THE COMPLEXITY OF THE PROBLEM

This chapter is intended to explain how chemicals weave their way into adolescent lives and why the abuse of chemicals in adolescence is complex and difficult to treat. Understanding this process does not imply that this abuse is condoned, nor does it minimize the seriousness of the problem. In fact, our goal is to highlight the negative effects such chemical abuse can have on the five areas of primary importance during the adolescent developmental process. These are: establishment of a separate identity, the heightening of the importance of peer relationships, the emergence of sexual awareness, the increase in cognitive powers, and the need to become productive.

Our behavior as human beings is influenced by our human needs. As infants and young children, most of our behavior is aimed toward getting other people to meet those needs for us. However, as we approach and enter adolescence, there is an expectation that we begin to meet these needs for ourselves so that we may mature into independent, self-sufficient adults. This can be an overwhelming realization for adolescents who are expected to become competent in many areas and who are not at all sure of their abilities to develop such competencies.

Adolescence is a time of high vulnerability. It represents the first major transitional period for a person, and it is approached with little wisdom, much impulsivity and, most important, no past success rate or experience with failure against which to measure oneself. Because of this, it can be an intensely stressful experience. The concern about whether one's needs will be met becomes paramount.

DRUGS APPEAR TO MEET KIDS' NEEDS

Unfortunately, for many young people, chemical use provides a false sense of achievement in meeting one's needs. The response to those needs from chemicals is quick and reliable. However, the problem is that chemical use distorts one's perceptions and allows for a form of self-deceit to take place. When this happens the adolescent can escape facing the challenge of developing the competencies and skills necessary to progress through life's stages. Personal development can become an illusion. The following discussion explores the ways in which chemicals provide this false sense of accomplishment.

ESTABLISHING A SEPARATE IDENTITY

The Ambivalence of Growing Up

Establishing a separate identity and achieving emotional and psychological independence from one's parents are needs in adolescence which provide for intense ambivalence. Adolescents recognize that they are unique and separate individuals, and they want this acknowledged. Generally, they want to be seen and treated as adults. On the other hand, adolescents desire the security and dependence of childhood. They want assurance that they will be unconditionally loved and cared for. Commonly, adolescents resent and blame their parents for these conflicting feelings. Resolution of these conflicts is a critical task and marks movement into adulthood. However, before this transition takes place, adolescents express ambivalence on a regular basis. This is demonstrated in the following exchange between an 18-year-old girl and her therapist (one of the authors):

> Girl: My boyfriend asked me to run away with him last week and get married. I really wanted to.
> Therapist: What kept you from going?
> Girl: I couldn't. I was grounded.

Drug Use as a Statement of Independence

Drug use is often seen by adolescents as a statement of independence when, in reality, it is a form of pseudo-independence. The intent of the use is frequently to display behavior that directly opposes that which is expected or demanded by authority figures. Adolescents exhibiting this behavior seem to be behaving independently and, at the same time, appear to be taking on adult behaviors such as drinking. In reality, they are dependent on knowing what is expected of them in order to do the opposite. The decision to act has not been freely derived through reflection but, rather, results from counter-dependent motivations. Thus, we see behavior which seems to indicate independence but which actually reflects another form of dependence.

Adding to this process is a conflictual parent-child relationship. While the adolescents who abuse chemicals are making "independent" statements by acting against their parents' wishes, they are at the same time forcing their parents to become involved in their lives rather than to appropriately separate. This is true because of the life-endangering nature of chemical abuse that literally demands parental involvement. For example, parents may want their adolescents to face the consequences of their own behavior such as paying legal fines resulting from driving while under the influence. However, when young people overdose or have serious accidents as the result of alcohol or drug abuse, parents are forced to take responsibility for dealing with this. These actions place parents in a decision-making bind. Stanton et al. (1978) refer to this dynamic as pseudo-individuation or pseudo-mutual independence.

A Sense of Self

As individuals move from childhood through adolescence, they begin to formulate a self-concept that gradually becomes clearer and more stable. Adolescents begin to define themselves in terms of specific skills, preferences, attributes and personality traits that are uniquely theirs. A personal identity based on what young people think about themselves emerges as these perceptions are consolidated into individual "self-portraits." At the same time, adolescents combine this information with an increased understanding of how they are seen by others. Most important, adolescents begin to evaluate, and hold personal opinions, about all of this.

Adolescents make judgments about themselves based on a number of factors. Often, these are not the same factors used by adults as standards in evaluating young people. For example, an adolescent who consistently gets good grades may be seen by her teachers as very successful. However, if this same young person has continual difficulty making friends, she may have low self-esteem. Self-concept is not objectively defined and, for the most part, it depends on the individual's perceptions, values and judgments.

Adults frequently do not understand why certain adolescents who, in adult eyes "have a lot going for them," do not feel good about themselves. Adolescents are involved in a process of intense self-scrutiny, and many tend to focus on personal flaws and deficits rather than on strengths. This often is not recognized by the adults in their lives.

Why do some adolescents have high self-esteem while others see themselves as unworthy failures? Extensive research on this question by Stanley Coopersmith (1967) has revealed four primary sources of self-esteem. These are reflected in how people assess their own success in life. Coopersmith has labeled these areas: power, significance, competence and virtue. What do these mean for the adolescent?

Power

Power is defined by Coopersmith as the ability to influence or control others. It is difficult for adolescents to maintain a positive sense of self if they feel that nothing they say or do makes any difference to anyone.

Young people need to experience a relationship between their actions and an effect on their world.

Research has shown that the need to experience environmental responses from personal actions is present from birth. Studies have shown that when this does not happen, infants suffer detrimental effects. In fact, Uzgiris and Hunt (1978) concluded in their explorations of infant development that "Living apathetically without response from the environment would be expected to result in retardation" (p. 23).

The need to feel an impact on one's world does not diminish as people get older. In adolescence it is particularly important. While young people are questioning the meaning of their existence, they are desperately seeking affirmation from those around them. They must face this basic question, "Does anything I do in my life truly make a difference?"

Adolescents who are unable to achieve a sense of power in positive, socially acceptable ways will often turn to deviant or destructive means. The act of vandalism is a prime example. Drug abuse and sexual promiscuity are others. With these acts the adolescent feels powerful and in control. Those who work with young people need to address the issue of how these adolescents can achieve a sense of power in our society in productive and constructive ways. Opportunities for this can occur in the family, the peer group, the school and the community. Ideally, individuals have chances to make a difference in all of these areas.

Significance

Significance is defined as the acceptance, attention and affection of others. These are needs that everyone has. These needs are especially important in adolescence, because the self-concept is at a relatively unstable developmental stage. Unfortunately, people who have little trouble recognizing these needs in young children frequently find them hard to acknowledge in adolescents. Adolescents themselves contribute to this. Because of their fear of rejection and humiliation, they do not easily show how much they really need affection, attention and acceptance. It is a challenge for those who live and work with young people to look beyond this.

Virtue

By virtue, Coopersmith refers to adherence to moral and ethical standards. Accomplishments in this area, on both the level of personal satisfaction and the level of societal recognition, enhance self-worth. Adolescents need opportunities to feel that they are contributing to a greater good or a cause which is beyond their own personal gratification. Schools, churches and community organizations can provide chances for this to happen.

It has been suggested by those who have studied the effects of school size on adolescent behavior (Barker and Gump, 1964) that smaller schools socially benefit students to a greater extent than larger ones do. This is because in these schools there are fewer students available to fill a given number of the roles necessary to maintain the function of the school. In smaller schools students are clearly needed. In contrast, larger schools make it possible for only a minority of the school population to be involved in running the school. In these schools there are more students who lose the opportunity to fully participate in the functions of the school. Because of this, many feel the effects of being left out.

Competence

Competence is reflected in successful performance in meeting demands for achievement. When young people have the experience of effectively attaining personal goals, their self-concept is greatly enhanced. They feel competence when they know they have met a challenge.

Working toward goals involves risking failure and, for many adolescents, this risk keeps them from attempting to even set goals. These young people would rather not have any goals than have to face the possibility of failure. In addition, many adolescents have not learned to set realistic goals. This is a skill that people are most likely to learn if they have had the opportunity to experience a feeling of competence in some area. This allows the person to establish a standard against which to gauge potential. Consistent experiences with failure inhibit this process. Those who work with adolescents can help build self-confidence in these young people by providing challenges for them that do not overextend their abilities.

The four factors outlined above are crucial elements in the formation of high self-esteem in adolescents. Young people may turn to drugs when one or more of these factors are not positively present in their lives. Low self-worth often contributes to adolescents moving from experimentation with drugs to drug abuse and dependence.

THE HEIGHTENING OF PEER RELATIONSHIPS

During adolescence, acceptance by one's peers is of primary importance. These peers provide standards by which adolescents compare themselves and others. Interactions with peers provide socialization experiences which are crucial to one's development. Peers are of critical importance during the adolescent period. As young people experience the need to separate from the primary adults in their lives, they also experience the fear, loneliness and alienation of not being able to turn to them for nurturance and support. Peers become a natural and safe source of this support. During adolescence, exposure beyond the family, primarily through one's peers, broadens the perspectives of adolescents and paves the way for these young people to separate from their parents. Part of this process involves the development of the ability to form intimate relationships. Developing intimacy in relationships involves both success, which results in acceptance, and failure, which results in rejection. Healthy adolescents reflect maturity when they are able to manage both. This is, therefore, a highly threatening time for adolescents due to the risk of rejection. However, movement through this phase is crucial in forming the basis of later intimate relationships. (Peer relationships are discussed further in Chapter Four.)

Instant Intimacy Through a Drug-Using Culture

Chemical use during adolescence provides a "ready-made" peer group: that of the drug-using culture. The primary vehicle for socialization in this group is the use of drugs. This peer group provides a sense of belonging through common dress, language, values and attitudes. It also provides "instant intimacy" with behaviors that imitate intimacy but which do not carry the risk and threat involved in truly intimate relationships.

Also, adolescents very quickly develop intimate relationships with chemicals themselves, looking to them for the constancy and reliability attributed to personal relationships. Adolescents who turn to chemicals to meet the intimacy need never experience the element of risk inherent in relationships and never fully understand the boundaries of their own vulnerability. Therefore, because of the constant fear of rejection, they become less and less able to develop mature adult relationships.

THE EMERGENCE OF SEXUAL AWARENESS

Physical Changes

No aspect of adolescent development is more readily apparent than that of the onset of puberty. The accompanying physical changes are dramatically evident to everyone, particularly to the person experiencing them. These changes are assessed and commented on, resulting in an intense self-consciousness on the part of the adolescent. Each adolescent lives through these years in anticipation of the outcome of these physical changes. There is a pressing need to see oneself as, and to be seen as, "normal." This is particularly difficult to accomplish during adolescence for a number of reasons. A primary one is that there is vast diversity in physical sizes and shapes within even a small age range. Anyone who has attended an eighth-grade basketball game can attest to this. These differences are a result of differences in the timing of maturity, but they also reflect factors such as heredity, nutrition, and lifestyle.

An additional barrier to the positive accomplishment of this developmental task is the adolescent view that equates "normality" with perfection, and the unrealistic expectation that if perfection is not attainable then one must accept being totally unacceptable. Adolescents find it hard to find a middle ground here. If they do not fit a very narrowly defined ideal, they become highly self-critical. They often become obsessed with what they see as their physical flaws and imperfections.

The need for finding comfort with these physical changes is further exacerbated by the hormonal changes which can be very disturbing for adolescents. These changes result in concerns about menstruation and breast size for girls, and worries about nocturnal emissions and spontaneous erections for boys. In addition, rapid changes in physical development, combined with generalized self-consciousness, cause adolescents to move in ways that are frequently seen as awkward or clumsy.

Insecurity related to one's emerging body image in adolescence is largely a result of the fact that the future is unknown. Adolescents may look to their parents for some idea about how they will look when mature, and this may or may not provide some relief, but it certainly is not clearly predictive. In addition, the media presents a very narrow view of what one should look like. It is not surprising that eating disorders in adolescence are common and are relatively difficult to treat. The fact that a number of adolescent girls have literally killed themselves through not eating demonstrates the intensity of this issue for adolescents.

The use of chemicals alleviates, for the adolescent, the extreme stress associated with the self-consciousness they feel about their physical appearance. It also allows them to excuse clumsiness and awkwardness as a side effect of the chemical use or to avoid awareness of it. In addition, this chemical use provides relief from the stresses associated with hormonal imbalance and provides a way for adolescents to self-medicate.

The Sexual Conflict

As adolescents become sexually mature on the physical level, they also begin to grapple with the meaning of sexual maturity on the social level. This creates conflict because of the many mixed messages adolescents are exposed to regarding this issue. As Gregory (1978) has stated, "Their interest in the opposite sex intensifies as they become sexually mature, yet their need for sexual fulfillment is discouraged by the restraints and taboos set by society." It is clear that these restraints and taboos have diminished significantly in recent years. However, there are still many real concerns that must be addressed. These include religious influences, beliefs about pregnancy and abortion, and worries about diseases including AIDS. There are no clear answers for today's adolescent.

This upheaval known as the "sexual revolution" has caused even greater conflict for adolescents. As Ingersoll (1982) has noted, "Society as a whole tends to have a much more permissive attitude about premature sexual activity." However, he points out that "premature commitment may interfere with the satisfactory resolution of other developmental tasks."

McCreary-Juhasz (1975) has suggested that there has been a shift from the influence of society to a focus on the individual as the decision maker regarding sexual activity. This places even greater stress on the adolescent. Wanting so desperately to be normal, they ask, "What is normal?" They will receive dramatically different answers from friends, parents, teachers, counselors, religious leaders, the media and literature.

Chemicals Reduce the Conflict

This conflict regarding sexual behavior is greatly reduced by the use of chemicals as are the inhibitions, both internal and external, that accompany that conflict. Thus, the sexual "acting out" that may occur because of chemical abuse has a destructive potential. This is because it is a behavior resulting not from reflection and awareness but rather from a "masking" of the issue. Sexual activity while under the influence of chemicals results in conflicts in values and concerns about values not adhered to. An inherent danger lies in adolescents' need to reduce this additional stress through continued use of alcohol or drugs. The abuse of chemicals provides an escape from confronting the issues, and because of this, it also retards the adoelscent's development and growth in this area as well.

INCREASED COGNITIVE POWERS

The Development of Abstract Thinking

In addition to being a time of profound physical change, adolescence is also a time when cognitive functioning goes through dramatic changes. The most widely recognized change is the appearance of formal operational thought where concrete operational thought once prevailed. This increase in the ability to think abstractly allows adolescents to reflect on, and make independent judgments about, their experience. They take a philosophic and idealistic view of society and begin to express strong opinions about what is "just" and what is "fair." Hurlock (1973) has cited studies showing that adolescents spend a good deal of time discussing with one another issues such as religion, the nature of God, and the meaning of life.

In addition, adolescents begin to consider alternatives and to develop a personal ideology, and they begin to experience conflict with adults who do not share their desire to correct all the social wrongs in the world. Because of their adolescent egocentrism (often seen by adults as self-centeredness), they do not understand that adults may not be as interested in their thoughts and ideas as they themselves are. Adults, in fact, may find the "know-it-all" attitude of the adolescent irritating. The egocentrism or self-centeredness of adolescents changes as they develop and acquire a different world view. This can be a struggle for them, however, as the following example illustrates.

Sandy, a 16-year-old girl, had been treated for alcoholism and was progressing well in her treatment. She wanted to go out dancing as she had in her "drinking days" but was stopped by her fear that everyone would be looking at her while she danced. She genuinely believed that all eyes would be on her as she danced, and the pressure for her was intense. This attitude represents a view held by most children and many adolescents. As we mature into adults, we learn that the world does not exist solely to provide an audience for us and we become less self-conscious.

In the past, Sandy had resolved this internal conflict, a developmental challenge, artificially through the use of alcohol. Now she was encouraged to face the challenge by going out dancing without the use of alcohol. Success at doing this provided an important landmark for her. She learned that she could enjoy dancing without drinking, and, most important, she matured beyond the child's-eye view of herself as the center of the universe.

As can be seen through this example, the self-centeredness of adolescence contributes to extreme self-consciousness. Most adolescents resolve this through living through some painful and uncomfortable experiences. Others, like Sandy, turn to alcohol or drugs to alleviate the tension and stress. Using chemicals in this way is harmful because it keeps the adolescent from actually resolving the conflict. Sandy was successful at this resolution only after she stopped using alcohol.

Interference of Drugs in the Thinking Process

The adaptation to these increased cognitive powers can cause increased conflict within the adolescent because of the challenge presented and the desire for the more simple times of childhood when things were seen in black-and-white, either/or terms. The use of drugs provides an experience in which adolescents can artificially achieve intellectual abstraction. Discussions while under the influence of drugs (marijuana in particular) are usually quite abstract but have little substance. This pseudo-intellectual "think talk" gives the illusion that it reflects advanced thinking. In reality, the behavior is an imitation.

In addition, the adolescent who moves into a heavy pattern of drug use, usually not attending school, or attending while high, misses the academic structure which is designed to stimulate the development of abstract thought. This further compounds the problem.

Language and the Subculture

The subculture of those who use drugs has a unique language (often later adopted by other adolescents). A characteristic of this language is its generalizability. Adolescents use one word to mean many things. "I freaked out," for example, can mean "I was the happiest I've ever been," or "I almost died." The use of these non-specific words reinforces the lag between cogitive development and language development during adolescence. Elkind (1967) has suggested that adolescents are more intellectually capable than their language indicates and that they need to learn to express themselves meaningfully through language. Adolescents in a drug-using peer group, who perhaps are also not attending school, isolate themselves from this challenge. Chemical use during adolescence inhibits intellectual development.

IMPORTANCE OF BECOMING PRODUCTIVE

Realizing Potential

The final goal of adolescence is the movement away from the total non-productive dependence of childhood into the productive and self-sustaining independence of adulthood. Adolescents must develop an accurate perspective of their abilities and how they fit into society's needs. We begin to see this in the healthy development of adolescents as they become active in school activities, obtain jobs, assume household responsibilities and begin making mature decisions. For example, adolescents who participate in team sports have opportunities to experience goal setting, self-discipline, cooperation and their own physical potential. Adolescents who work on the yearbook gain skills in organization and in accepting and delegating responsibility. In addition, they are both creatively and intellectually stimulated.

Chemical-abusing adolescents become "productive" in a drug-using culture. Most of their resources, in terms of energy or commitment, are focused on obtaining and using chemicals. These young people rarely obtain the experience needed to realize their own potential and possibilities. Being productive is defined in terms of assuring drug availability or amount used.

The Destructive Cycle

Adolescents are particularly subject to substance abuse problems and chemical dependence as the skills needed to move through the transition to adulthood are themselves in a developmental stage. Chemicals provide a reliable, albeit dysfunctional, vehicle to meet these developmental needs. The use of chemicals keeps young people from experiencing the challenges which are necessary for developing important skills. The further adolescents fall behind developmentally, the more they look to chemicals to provide the relief needed to resolve the crisis resulting from such a deficit. Thus, a downwardly spiralling cycle occurs, and what once was considered a fun and recreational activity has become a destructive process.

In the areas of adolescent development discussed in this chapter, the use of chemicals in adolescence may help adolescents meet many of their needs. However, in so doing, the developmental process is distorted so that the adolescent becomes, in effect, "retarded" in their socialization. It is the experience of these authors that an adolescent who has been regularly using chemicals for two years will typically be undersocialized and developmentally behind by no less than two years. The use of chemicals appears to be the easy way out, but, in reality, it makes things more difficult for individual personal growth and development.

Because of the complexity of the process, and the interaction of the factors discussed in this chapter, it can be seen that it can be helpful for those who work with young people to view adolescent chemical abuse as a need-meeting process. The challenge is to facilitate ways in which adolescents can meet those needs and developmental tasks in healthy, appropriate and skill-building ways. The following chapters will address this issue and will suggest strategies for working with adolescents based on these assumptions.

CHAPTER THREE

ASSESSMENT OF THE PROBLEM

Adolescent drug or alcohol abuse is probably the most commonly missed major pe-diatric diagnosis. For every child in treatment, there are many, many more whose disease continues to progress because it is never diagnosed, only partially diagnosed, or diagnosed too late.

(Macdonald, 1984)

ADOLESCENT ASSESSMENTS

AN ASSESSMENT determines the likelihood that alcohol or other drugs are causing problems in an adolescent's life. The severity of those problems, along with the duration, frequency, and amount of use, determines the seriousness of the problem and has implications for the plan of intervention and treatment.

Most parents and many professionals who refer adolescents for an assessment want the answer to one question and that question is, "Is this young person chemically dependent?" While a thorough assessment can provide such a diagnosis, this answer alone is of limited utility. Recommendations for treatment programs are based on a number of factors which must also be considered and which are discussed in this chapter.

A diagnosis of chemical dependency implies the need for the adolescent to be involved in some sort of treatment program, ususally on an inpatient basis, initially. However, it is important to note here that other diagnoses such as chemical misuse or abuse also indicate the need for some intervention and/or treatment. In these cases the recommendation is usually for treatment on an outpatient basis. The diagnosis itself is not as important as the determination of a relationship between the adolescent's life circumstances and the use of alcohol or drugs. Each

37

adolescent's unique situation must be taken into account in planning a treatment program based on the assessment.

Where Do Assessments Begin?

Assessments ideally begin wherever someone has contact with an adolescent and views symptoms in the adolescent that may be related to alcohol or drug usage.

Schools

Schools can be the ideal place for assessments and interventions to occur. It is the environment where the adolescent spends the greatest amount of waking hours. The school therefore is in the position of witnessing change or stability over time, a critical component of an assessment. (Refer to Chapter Five for additional discussion of the school's role.) Assessments in the school can be made by trained school personnel or by professionals from treatment centers who can come to the school for the assessment or who can have the adolescent come to the treatment center. We recommend that the initial assessment take place at the school, if possible, because this is less threatening to the adolescent and the information gathered is more likely to be accurate.

Juvenile Courts

Research indicates that a large percentage of youth who come through the juvenile court system have substance abuse problems (Halikas et al., 1984). Identifying these adolescents at the point of entry into the system and making a referral to a treatment center for an assessment, with subsequent appropriate treatment, could prevent this adolescent from re-entering the juvenile court system at a later date.

Physicians

Adolescent drug or alcohol abuse is one of the most frequently missed major pediatric problems (Macdonald, 1984).

> Adolescent drug abuse is a major disease seen regularly by pediatricians, but diagnosed infrequently. The reasons for missing the diagnosis are multiple, but for the affected teenager and his family, such error may be disastrous. Suspecting the diagnosis but delaying therapy or referring for ineffective treatment is a common and serious problem.
> The teenager who comes to a pediatric office because of fatigue, cough, sore throat, red eyes, chest pain, or other unexplained symptoms may have a drug problem. It is no longer adequate to do labora-

tory work for infectious mononucleosis, anemia, and hepatitis and not consider drugs as a possible cause of fatigue. If the child's lethargy is too quickly blamed on insufficient sleep, an overly busy schedule, or mild adolescent withdrawal, the real cause of the problem may be missed. (p. 1)

Community Centers

Community centers traditionally are gathering places for adolescents during after-school hours. Adolescents typically relax and are quite candid with youth workers in these agencies. They are likely to share stories about drug and alcohol using with the youth workers, and they may show symptoms which a critical eye can detect. Workers at community centers can then refer these adolescents to a treatment center for an assessment.

Mental Health Agencies

Adolescents and their families come to mental health and social service agencies with a variety of problems. A common problem is an acting-out adolescent and parents who present themselves as lacking any influence over their child. In these cases, the potential exists for a drug or alcohol abuse problem to be related to this presenting problem. Given that the denial of substance use and abuse by adolescents is quite high, a mental health setting can be an ideal starting point for an assessment. This is because it may be seen as less threatening to the adolescent than a drug and alcohol treatment facility is.

Emergency Rooms

Intoxicated adolescents are seen in hospital emergency rooms and are treated either for an overdose or the result of an accidental injury incurred while under the influence. It is advisable and in the best interest of the adolescent and the family if some referral for assessment and follow-up occur in these cases. A study of 171 acutely intoxicated adolescents admitted to the emergency department of a hospital demonstrated that the general hospital with a 24-hour emergency room can play a vital role not only in the crisis management of intoxicated adolescents but in their follow-up, assessment and, when indicated, appropriate referral for outside assessment and treatment (Stephenson et al., 1984).

The Multidisciplinary Team Approach

An effective assessment brings together as many perspectives as possible. A quality assessment includes opinions from a team of individuals representing a variety of areas of expertise. This should also include people, such as school personnel, who know the adolescent in other situations.

The Primary Assessor

The primary assessor, or case manager as some agencies prefer to call this person, is responsible for gathering all the information about the adolescent. Information is gathered from other members of the team, and from the adolescent, through one or more interviews. The primary assessor makes a determination about the severity of the problem by examining the relationship between the adolescent's use of alcohol and drugs and the problems which are present in that young person's life.

The Physician

The physician determines the impact of the adolescent's alcohol or drug use on his or her physical health. This may take place through physical examinations, interviews and laboratory tests.

The Family Therapist

The family therapist considers the entire family constellation and the dynamics within the family, and assesses the role that the adolescent's alcohol or drug use plays in the family situation. A thorough family assessment can help in the identification of other related problems as well. (See Chapter Four and the section on "Family Therapy" in Chapter Seven.)

The Psychiatrist or Psychologist

Psychiatric or psychological evaluations can be extremely helpful in the assessment process. They can help determine the presence of underlying personality problems or pathological conditions that may be difficult to detect in an initial interview.

School Personnel

Teachers, school social workers, guidance counselors and school administrators all have important observed and documented performance data on their students (see Chapter Five). This information can be used in determining if there is a connection between the adolescent's alcohol and drug use and his or her performance at school.

School personnel can also provide useful information about possible adjustment difficulties they may have noted and the onset of an adolescent's alcohol or drug problem.

The assessment procedure is greatly enhanced by a team approach utilizing as much information as possible.

Conducting the Assessment

The goal of an assessment with an adolescent is twofold: (1) the determination of whether alcohol or drugs are causing problems in the adolescent's life; and (2) intervention in a way that motivates the adolescent to change his or her behavior. The assessment can then be a process of gathering information as well as of mutual problem solving. The information that is obtained in determining the nature of the problem can be used, in turn, to provide feedback to the adolescent in such a way that it promotes some action on the part of the young person.

A thorough assessment consists of three parts which are ideally conducted by the same individual. (If they are not conducted by the same interviewer, one person should be assigned the task of gathering and organizing this information.) These parts include the adolescent interview, the family interview and collateral interviews. Collateral interviews may include interviews with school personnel, social service representatives and legal authorities who may be involved in the case.

An assessment procedure that includes as many perspectives as possible will describe a more complete picture of the adolescent, and will be more likely to be accurate, than one that focuses on just one person's view of the situation. For these reasons, it is highly recommended that time and effort be made to interview as many involved people as possible.

Accuracy in the assessment process is also enhanced by honesty on the part of the adolescents being interviewed. If adolescents see the interviewer as someone who understands their view of the world, they are more likely to give truthful information and to participate in developing a plan for change. A basic level of rapport and trust can usually be established by acknowledging the adolescent's experience. For example, the interviewer might begin with a statement such as the following:

"You have been referred for an assessment. Most kids like you get pretty angry about this and I imagine that you might feel that way, too. I don't know whether or not you have a drug or alcohol problem. That is what I must determine, and to do that I'll have to ask you some questions. The results of this assessment are only as good as the information you give me. When I am finished with the interview, I would be glad to share my opinion with you if you want. I want to give you and others an accurate opinion and that will depend on the honesty of your answers."

The following guidelines are suggested for use during the rest of the interview:

1. Never assume before the interview that an adolescent does (or does not) have a problem with alcohol or drugs. Try to keep an open mind and evaluate facts and information in an objective, systematic manner.

2. Be gently but persistently probing and confrontive, and honestly point out inconsistencies, as well as facts that the adolescent may not want to hear. Remember that assessment interviews and procedures are prototypes for future counseling sessions. Beginnings are very important, as they set the stage and tone for what will follow.

3. Avoid getting sidetracked into discussing issues unrelated to alcohol or drug use. If you do, you are less likely to obtain the needed information, and you may be setting a precedent which is difficult to break later.

4. Be aware that denial will exist where there are drug or alcohol problems. However, it is not necessary to invariably expect or look for denial. (Interviews with significant others can aid a great deal in determining the extent of the client's denial.)

5. Refrain from judging the adolescent's drug or alcohol use or related behaviors. The adolescent will not benefit from moralistic or punitive attitudes or statements on the part of the counselor. It is important to accept the young person as he or she is right from the start and to let the adolescent experience your acceptance.

6. Make assessment and diagnosis a cooperative venture with the adolescent. Create an atmosphere and ongoing practice of working together, with the young person as an equal partner. Even though the adolescent may not appear to accept or even be interested in such a cooperative arrangement, it is essential that the offer be made.

7. Don't try to be a "detective" who is using hidden means to uncover or prove the adolescent's alcohol or drug problems. Be absolutely straightforward and direct in communicating to the client what it is that you hope to find out, and what you intend to do with that information.

8. Don't hurry diagnosis — a week or more can profitably be spent in dealing with diagnostic and assessment issues with the assessment team.
9. Pay attention to hunches and intuitions and follow them up. Some will prove illusory, but some will be accurate and valuable.

Special Considerations With Adolescents

There are well-established lists of signs and symptoms which are used in assessment of chemical dependency in adults (McAuliffe and McAuliffe, 1975). With adolescents, there are special considerations which must be taken into account in adapting these signs and symptoms (specific symptoms are discussed later in this chapter).

First, physical signs and symptoms are not as evident with adolescents as they are with adults. For example, conditions such as cirrhosis of the liver or severe withdrawal symptoms, frequently present in adults who have been abusing alcohol or drugs, are not regularly seen in adolescents. This is not to say that there are not some physical symptoms with adolescents, but an accurate assessment should include other documentation, as well, and the focus should be on behavioral data.

Second, adolescents are at a developmental stage where they may be isolated from the role performances expected of adults. While adults are accountable for their behavior in a number of areas such as work, family and friendships, and deterioration in this behavior might indicate a problem, adolescents are allowed more latitude. Poor performance by adolescents is often attributed to inexperience and, because of this, is tolerated and explained as a developmental stage. Drug and alcohol problems frequently fail to be recognized as possibly causal in these situations.

For example, adults who have consistent difficulty getting to work on time or who are increasingly unkempt in their appearance may be subject to suspicion about possible alcohol or drug abuse. Adolescents demonstrating the same problems with promptness or physical appearance are more likely to be excused or tolerated and the behavior attributed to normal adolescence. With adolescents, it is more difficult to differentiate potential problem behaviors from what may be the natural aversion to conformity often shown by young people in their attempts to be different.

Third, an assessment with adolescents must take into account the fact that adolescents are relatively inexperienced in the use of alcohol and other drugs. Because of this, they are both less physically able to tolerate alcohol and drugs and they are less skilled at compensating for the effects while under the influence. Signs and symptoms used to assess these factors for adults may need to be adapted for use with adolescents. For example, drinking to the point of passing out is a danger sign when it happens to a young person. However, it may indicate inexperience with the use of alcohol and does not necessarily indicate dependency. When drinking to passing out happens with adults, it almost always has serious implications.

Assessment Tools

Assessment tools such as structured questionnaires (see Appendix G) can be helpful in organizing information. However, they should not be relied on solely for determining the outcome of an adolescent assessment. A thorough assessment goes beyond the facts gathered by such instruments and includes a plan of intervention or treatment based upon each adolescent's unique situation. Assessment tools can be useful but are limited in accomplishing the overall goals of an assessment.

The Problem Continuum

As drug and alcohol use in an adolescent progress from no use through experimentation and social use and on to the more serious stages of misuse, abuse, and finally dependency, the problems evident in the adolescent's life also increase. Many beginners in adolescent assessment prefer to concentrate on the determination of how much or how often an adolescent is using alcohol or drugs. While such information is critical, the pattern of use alone does not determine dependency. A thorough and accurate assessment considers the pattern of use in light of the problems occurring in an adolescent's life. These problems are best viewed in terms of negative changes, including changes in performance, attitude, behavior and mood. It is the willingness of the individual to continue using alcohol or drugs and to risk the escalating consequences of that use that highlights the intensity of the alcohol or drug abuse or actual chemical dependency. The problem continuum can be a helpful visual tool in connecting problems with the level of use.

The assessment of chemical abuse or dependency among adolescents should be viewed as a flexible process. For example, drinking three to four beers per episode and drinking three to four times per week may produce varying consequences for different adolescents. For some, it

THE PROBLEM CONTINUUM

Drug/Alcohol Use Continuum	No Use	Experimentation	Social Use	Misuse	Abuse	Chemical Dependency
Problem Continuum	No problems	No problems; Parents perhaps aware due to drunkenness resulting from inexperience	Consequences may occur; life in general unaffected	Problems arise; changes evident	Problems increase; poor relationships and decline in performance in many areas of life	Multiple life problems; every area of life affected

may interfere greatly with school performance and attendance and perhaps result in a drunk-driving accident, or it may be related to a burglary. If this adolescent persists in drinking in spite of such consequences, he may most helpfully be diagnosed as chemically dependent.

On the other hand, another adolescent may progress to a point of drinking and smoking marijuana daily during the summer. Upon return to school in the fall he may notice difficulty in concentrating and may be suspended as a result of drinking on the premises. These two problems could be the impetus for this adolescent to stop drinking or using drugs in order to avoid the risk of any more serious problems. This adolescent would not be diagnosed as chemically dependent, even though daily use had been documented.

It is this process of the connection of life problems with the pattern of use that is at the core of a professional assessment. A thorough assessment not only determines a pattern of use but also assesses the relationship of drug or alcohol use to an adolescent's life. It is the relationship with, and the commitment to, the drugs and alcohol that determines whether or not an adolescent is chemically dependent. Focusing solely on amount and frequency of use does not get at this critical issue.

A Primary or Secondary Problem?

As we have mentioned, it is common for problems with alcohol or drug use in adolescents to be accompanied by other problems such as poor school performance, depression and attention-deficit disorders. It is frequently difficult to determine which seems to be causal. People who work with young people often ask, for example, is the young person depressed because of problems with alcohol and drugs, or is the depression causing the person to use chemicals as a way of dealing with it?

When there are multiple problems present in the life of an adolescent, it can be complicated to determine which are primary problems and which seem to be secondary. Initially, it is not necessary to decide this. What is more helpful in this process is to identify the problems and their effects and to establish a priority list for addressing each one.

Chemical dependency is usually addressed first in treatment programs, not because it is considered to be the cause of the other problems, but because it is important for the adolescent to be alcohol and drug free in order to deal with the other issues. Also, when the young person is not using alcohol or drugs, it is easier to examine the question of whether the problems associated with their use are primary or secondary.

The adolescent who progresses to experiencing serious life problems, and who demonstrates an inability to stop using alcohol or drugs, clearly will need a treatment program that addresses all issues in order for successful recovery to take place. The plans for intervention and treatment should take into consideration all aspects of the adolescent's life. In this way, a thorough assessment can be the first step in the resolution of those problems that are identified. The following case example demonstrates how this takes place: .

Tom was admitted to the hospital as a very withdrawn and noncommunicative 15-year-old. He had been using a variety of illicit drugs and alcohol daily for the past year and his erratic behavior was of concern to the treatment staff. After admission, he was gradually withdrawn from alcohol and the drugs he had been using. In response to this, he became almost catatonic, frequently curling into a fetal position and ignoring those around him. A thorough psychiatric evaluation with a psychiatrist, along with a complete psychological evaluation, revealed that Tom suffered from a serious underlying depression. A family social history revealed that Tom's father also suffered from a lifelong depression. In Tom's case the assessment did not result in viewing either the depression or the chemical dependency as more important than the other. Both problems were considered as co-existing primary problems and were treated as such.

After he was withdrawn physically from the drugs and alcohol he had been using, he became involved in an abstinence program in order to provide an alcohol- and drug-free state. Then, to address the depression, Tom was administered psychotropic medication and psychotherapy. Tom needed to be alcohol and drug free to respond to the prescribed medication effectively and to be an active participant in psychotherapy. In this case, the chemical dependency was viewed as a priority rather than as primary condition. This means that one issue needed to be addressed before the other, equally critical problem could be treated.

SYMPTOMS

As mentioned, an assessment is a process of gathering information about the adolescent's patterns of behavior that are related to substance abuse. These patterns of behavior are the symptoms. The following discussion defines the symptoms of chemical dependency and outlines basic behaviors. Also included are key questions which should be asked in order to obtain the information that is necessary for determining the severity of the problem.

Preoccupation

Preoccupation is an obsession with using alcohol or drugs and with getting high. A great deal of time is spent thinking about getting high, planning to get high, and planning how to procure alcohol and drugs in order to continue to get high.

A high school alcohol and drug counselor informally interviewed a group of chemically dependent adolescents he worked with. He asked them to estimate how many times during a class period (50 minutes) they thought about getting high or being high. They reported approximately 20 to 30 times per class period. Because of this, it can be seen that preoccupation is not only a symptom of dependency, it is also a critical barrier to learning. Adolescents who are dependent on alcohol or drugs are not going to be assimilating class material, and poor school achievement will result.

Another indicator of dependency is the level of risk adolescents are willing to assume in order to insure that they will be able to continue to get high. Some adolescents steal from parents and friends. Others shoplift or steal from students or teachers at their schools. Some are willing to burglarize, while many begin to sell drugs themselves. What is most important for the preoccupied adolescent is being high and staying high. The price that must be paid to achieve this becomes inconsequential.

Questions to Ask

1. Do you find yourself looking forward to the next time you can get high?
2. Do you look forward to the weekend so you can get high?
3. Do you find yourself thinking about getting high when you are supposed to be thinking about other things or doing other things?
4. Do you prefer to hang around with friends who also drink or use drugs?
5. Do you only go to parties where alcohol or drugs will be used?
6. Do you get high during the school day?
7. Do you think about getting high during classes?
8. How do you pay for alcohol or drugs?
9. Have you ever stolen or shoplifted for money to buy drugs?
10. Have you ever burglarized homes for cash, liquor, drugs or items to sell?

11. Have you ever sold drugs?
12. Do you ever drink or use drugs before going out in order to be sure that you will get high enough?

Increased Tolerance

As tolerance for a specific substance builds, the body must take in more of that substance to achieve the same euphoric effect that lesser amounts previously achieved. At the same time, the body's ability to tolerate larger amounts of the substance increases as well.

Adolescents seem to develop increased tolerance more quickly than adults do. This is usually demonstrated by the pride that many adolescents take in being able to consume large quantities of either alcohol or drugs. The assessment of tolerance can be made through gathering information about the adolescent's alcohol and drug use history (see Appendix G).

Questions to Ask

1. How much can you drink (or smoke, or consume) before you pass out?
2. Do you frequently find that you drink (or use drugs) more than your friends do?
3. Have your friends commented on how you hold your liquor (or handle your drug use)?
4. Are you proud of your ability to drink (or use drugs) so much?

Blackouts

A blackout is a period of time during which a person simply does not remember what happened. It occurs while drinking and the person is alert and conscious. It is not passing out.

After blackouts people may remember what happened both before and after the episode. However, they will not be able to recall where they were, who they were with, or what they did during the time of the blackout.

A blackout is one of the most critical symptoms of alcoholism. Blackouts are not present in cases of drug dependency without alcoholism, and occur only in cases of alcoholism or alcoholism with drug dependency.

During assessments it is often necessary to explain the difference between a blackout and passing out to adolescents. This is a symptom that frequently needs to be explained and discussed.

When confronted with information suggesting they may have experienced a blackout, many adolescents respond with surprise, confusion or extreme anger.

Questions to Ask

1. Have you ever had a difficult time remembering how you got home after drinking?
2. In the morning, after drinking, have you ever been unable to remember an entire period of time from the night before?
3. (If yes to either of the above) How many times has this happened?

Loss of Control

Traditionally, loss of control is viewed as the inability to stop drinking or using drugs once a person has used even a minimal amount. The old "one-drink-leads-to-twenty" syndrome comes to mind. While this can be true for adolescents, the concept of loss of control is more complex. Loss of control for adolescents refers to the inability to control the role that alcohol and other drugs play in their lives. It is exemplified by not being able to control how much is used in a given situation. For example, an adolescent who vows to only have one beer after school but comes home five hours later intoxicated, demonstrates loss of control.

We see loss of control in the adolescent who begins to realize there is a problem with his use, promises only to drink or use drugs on Saturday nights, and suddenly finds himself with a joint in his mouth on the way to school.

Loss of control is also evident in the inability of adolescents to predict the outcome of their use. The adolescent who is in trouble with the law and burglarizes a home while intoxicated, risking incarceration, demonstrates loss of control. As part of the inability to control the role alcohol or other drugs have in their lives, adolescents who are chemically dependent get high to avoid the letdown when sober.

Questions to Ask

1. Have you ever been unable to stop drinking or using drugs once you started?
2. Do you find yourself questioning how you got into some trouble when you promised yourself you would not do it again?

3. Do you sometimes drink or use drugs more than you should?
4. Do you make promises to yourself or others about how much you will drink or use drugs and then break those promises?
5. Do you ever feel like your life is out of control?
6. Do you find that you drink or use drugs because you are afraid of feeling bad if you don't?

Denial

Denial refers to the inability of chemically dependent adolescents to see and accept that there are serious problems in their lives and that these problems are directly related to their alcohol and drug use. Part of their denial involves attributing positive qualities to their drug experience at a point when the chemical use is no longer fun. Denial serves to keep adolescents from changing their behavior and giving up their chemical use.

For adolescents, the motivation to persevere in drinking or using drugs, in spite of serious consequences, can also be related to their immaturity. Part of the adolescent struggle involves wanting to become independent, and chemically dependent adolescents usually realize they are not there yet. They compensate by withdrawing from parents in an attempt to be grown up. To admit to a problem with alcohol or drugs requires giving up control and giving it back over to their parents. This is a frightening thought to adolescents who want no one in control of their lives but themselves.

Questions to Ask

1. Do you think that your use of alcohol or other drugs is causing the problems you are having?
2. What needs to happen in your life for your life to improve?

In assessing an adolescent's level of denial, it is not as important to ask questions as to assess the adolescent's reactions to questions and information. Adolescents who are in denial about their problems are frequently angry, sullen and hostile. They often blame teachers in school for their school problems, or dismiss school problems as unimportant because they hate school and have no intention of obtaining a degree. They minimize their problems by describing their parents as hysterical and overreacting.

Lying can also be an indication of denial. Adolescents who lie about what they use, how much, and how often is attempting to "buy time" to time" to continue drinking or using drugs. Lying can be determined by a number of drug and alcohol histories being taken at different points by different interviewers. Chemically dependent adolescents frequently make mistakes in their stories as they are repeated, and sometimes even contradict their stories in the same interview. Multiple history taking can provide a number of checks and balances.

Using Large Quantities With Greater Frequency

A thorough drug and alcohol history is obtained to determine the frequency and amount of alcohol or drug use going on in the adolescent's life. A profile of the adolescent's use is developed by obtaining specific information for each drug used. Increases in amount used and movement toward daily use both indicate a problem that may have progressed to dependency.

Questions to Ask

1. What do you like to use most?, second, third, etc.
2. Have you ever used . . .? (Here, any drugs unnamed by the adolescent are mentioned.) For alcohol and each drug the following questions are asked:
3. How old were you when you first used this drug?
4. How old were you when you first became intoxicated?
5. When did you begin using this drug monthly, weekly, daily?
6. How many times per day do you use this drug?
7. How do you use it (drink, smoke, inhale, inject, freebase)?
8. What was the longest period of time you have experienced without chemicals, and what was that like?
9. When was the last time you used this drug?
10. Are you high right now?

(Refer to Appendix G for a guide for gathering information.)

Life Problems

An assessment details all the various life problems that an adolescent may be experiencing. Questions are asked and information is gathered relative to school performance, legal problems and pending issues, family problems, and suicidal ideation and gestures. When problems are noted in any of these areas, it is important to note when they occurred so that they may be related to the alcohol and drug use pattern. This assists in the determination of whether the alcohol or drug use problem is primary or secondary in the life of the adolescent.

SUICIDE AND ASSESSMENT

With suicide now ranking as the second leading cause of adolescent death (Grande et al., 1986), this issue cannot be ignored by those who work with adolescents in any setting, particularly treatment centers for chemically dependent young people. In a study of 133 cases of suicide by individuals younger than 30, 53 percent were found to meet the diagnostic criteria for substance abuse. The study concluded that increasing drug use in our society is part of the reason youth suicide rates have increased, and suggests that suicide can actually be a late stage of chemical dependency (Fowler et al., 1986).

This has implications for assessment. An assessment for chemical or alcohol dependency is not complete without also conducting an assessment for suicide risk. Adolescents are questioned about whether they have either considered suicide or have attempted to take their own life. Both reported considerations and attempts are probed further in the interview. The difference between a low risk and high risk for suicide is related to past attempts, proximity of the means, degree of hopelessness and the development of a plan. The following questions can be asked to assist in determining the risk for suicide (Grande et al., 1986):

1. How will you do it?
2. How much do you want to die?
3. How much do you want to live?
4. How often do you have these thoughts?
5. When you are thinking of suicide, how long do the thoughts stay with you?
6. Is there anyone or anything that could stop you?
7. Have you attempted suicide?
8. Do you have a plan?
9. On a scale of one to ten, what is the probability that you will kill yourself?
10. What happens that makes life worth living?
11. Are you more likely to consider taking your life before, during or after using drugs or alcohol?
12. Do you think being high or drunk might help you follow through with suicide?

13. Were you unhappy with life before you began using alcohol or drugs?

For some adolescents, drinking or using drugs is a means by which they carry out their suicide. In these cases, they either eventually "accidentally" overdose or are killed through some other alcohol or drug-induced accident. Others more intentionally and directly use alcohol or drugs to kill themselves, deliberately overdosing.

It is important to point out, however, that all depressed adolescents who use alcohol or drugs are not necessarily suicidal. In fact, many of these adolescents use chemicals to self-medicate. That is, they drink or use drugs to alleviate the psychological pain they are experiencing. An effective assessment procedure can help to differentiate these adolescents from those who are suicidal. Appropriate interventions can then be planned.

A SPECIAL ISSUE: ADOLESCENT CHILDREN OF CHEMICALLY DEPENDENT PARENTS

It is a known and accepted fact that children of chemically dependent parents are at high risk for substance abuse problems themselves (McDermott, 1984). While there is not a causal relationship and one cannot be certain that an adolescent child of a chemically dependent parent will necessarily be chemically dependent, the risk should not be ignored during the assessment process.

Information is obtained during the assessment process relative to dependency or drinking problems in the family. It is helpful to obtain this information about parents and both sets of grandparents. The following questions can help organize this information:

1. Is anyone in your family alcoholic or chemically dependent?
2. Has anyone in your family ever received treatment for an alcohol or drug problem?

It is not necessarily critical to determine whether or not family members are alcoholics. The accuracy of this information may be questionable due to the fact that a diagnosis results from an analysis of multiple criteria such as blackouts, work problems and others that may not be available to the adolescent. It is at times advisable to ask adolescents directly how they have been affected by parental drinking. The perception of parental drinking by the adolescent is quite influential. The following questions may be asked to determine this impact:

1. Do family members talk about a certain person's drinking as if it should be stopped, or as if they are ashamed of it?
2. Are you concerned about your parents' drinking or drug using?
3. Do you wish anyone in your family would not drink so much?
4. Do you think things would improve in your family if your mother or father would not drink so much?

Being the child of an alcoholic or of problem drinkers or drug users does not determine that a child will have a chemical or alcohol problem. But it does have some serious implications which are helpful to consider during the assessment process.

Adolescent children of alcoholic parents may have a distorted view of what "normal" drinking is. Because of this, they may not be able to identify what goes on in their homes as abusive drinking, and they may not have realistic standards for judging what is acceptable or unacceptable behavior related to the use of alcohol.

Other adolescents in such homes may recognize the problem drinking that is going on and may as a result vow never to drink themselves. When they break this vow, the guilt and fear is tremendous. Often, to assuage the guilt, they use alcohol, creating a cycle of use that is very difficult to break.

The chemically dependent adolescent who comes from this type of environment presents other challenges to those in treatment programs. Family members may not be able to tolerate the changes that will take place, since these changes may bring the focus of attention to the abusing parent or parents. Parents may sabotage their children's treatment program by not providing the support necessary for recovery. They may actually encourage or allow the adolescent to drink or use drugs, or they may refuse to be involved in the treatment program in any way. Initially, they may not be willing to help with the assessment by either not providing needed information or by minimizing the problem.

Some children of alcoholics develop symptoms of abuse and dependency very early in their drinking experience as illustrated by the following case example:

Allison was referred for an assessment by personnel at her school who had been concerned about her. At the time of the assessment, she indicated that she had been drinking for the past two months. She reported drinking approximately four to five beers at any one time. What was alarming about this assessment was that Allison revealed that she had already experienced a number of blackouts. The fact that Allison's father was an alcoholic contributed to the concern of those involved in the assessment. This assessment provided an opportunity to discuss with Allison the fact that she was at high risk for serious problems with alcohol and/or drugs. Also, it was recommended that Allison participate in a treatment program of a more intensive nature than might have been recommended were it not for the blackouts and the history of family alcoholism.

SUMMARY

Effective assessments of adolescents with alcohol and drug problems consider a variety of factors. Duration, frequency and amount of use of chemicals are important, but this information provides only part of the picture. Other problems which are present in the adolescent's life are critical indicators of the severity of the problem, also. These include problems which may be present in a number of settings including the school and the family. Comprehensive assessments involve examining both the history and the context of alcohol and drug use. They are designed to provide not only information but also a plan for intervention and/or treatment. (Chapter Seven deals extensively with treatment of the problem.)

CHAPTER FOUR

PEERS AND SOCIETY

Friendship, like anything else, can be cultivated or handled ineptly . . . Teens who cannot enjoy basketball turn to breaking windows; teens who can't cope with losses turn to cocaine; teens who have nothing to say to a friend turn to more risky sexual involvement.

(Csikszentmihalyi and Larson, 1984)

PEERS

Peer Pressure

ASK ANY GROUP of parents what they believe to be the primary cause of adolescent drug problems and the most common answer you will hear is "peer pressure." One obvious reason for this response is that it is often, understandably, difficult for parents to accept that they themselves may be part of the problem. Beyond that, and contributing to this view, are the facts that most adolescent drug use occurs with peers and that young people who use drugs tend to associate with other young people who use drugs (Jalali et al., 1981). It is a logical step to arrive at the conclusion that the culprit is peer pressure. Frequently, parents say, "She was just fine until she started hanging around with . . . That's when all the problems started." And, it often seems that way. However, the situation is usually more complicated and, while peer influences are important for reasons discussed in this chapter, adolescent problems are often the result of many factors, including peer pressure, which interact with one another. It is helpful to keep this in mind as we focus on the topic.

57

The Shift to Peers

There is an important shift that takes place as the developing child enters adolescence. When this happens, peers play a crucial role. Before the shift, parental figures provide the primary base of evaluation and judgment for the young person. Younger children usually share their parents' views about what is desirable and unacceptable, good and bad, and right and wrong.

At adolescence, a change begins to occur and the opinions of peers become the focus. This is especially true where the concerns are more concrete, such as those related to physical appearance and personal habits. The way that young people choose to, literally, present themselves to the world becomes determined, more and more, by peers. If they receive positive judgments from their friends about how they look, this carries much more weight than the evaluation made by parents. In fact, it is common for parents to disapprove of many of the choices that young people make about their appearance.

Because of the high visibility of the effects of peer influence in the lives of adolescents, involved adults often have difficulty. Their concern often centers around this question: If these young people are discarding adult values in some areas, how can we be sure it won't happen in others?

When peer identification becomes evident through physical signs and behaviors, parents are frequently very threatened. It is small consolation to consider that parental influence will show up in the future and that peer influence is basically oriented to the here and now. Most long-range plans, decisions and values are determined by family influence. In the meantime, however, peer pressure prevails and this is the source of much conflict in the family.

When adolescents listen to music that their parents find weird at best and immoral at worst, when these young people speak a language that is very much their own, and when they choose to dress in ways that parents find unacceptable, the seeds are planted for potential problems. An adolescent whose unusual hairstyle is protested by a parent says, "Look, it's *my* hair!" while the parents are asking, "Where will this end?"

Their Own Culture

In the time that they spend together, which in our society is substantial, with adolescents spending a full half of their waking hours with peers, adolescents create a culture of their own. This culture is quite different from the culture of their parents.

Whether parents like it or not, for most adolescents, friends have moved to the forefront and interest in the family is on the wane. What purpose do these peer relationships serve in the life of an adolescent?

Adolescent peers help one another develop an identity separate from the family. These young people share their own views of the world, unique norms and behaviors and common experiences. Also, they provide support for one another in their struggle to break away from the family, as well as challenge to negotiate relationships in the group. They find comfort in dressing like their friends. Conformity to a peer group is one of the tools young people use to make bearable the process of separating from adults.

The association with a group of peers provides the groundwork for adolescents to eventually leave home. The development of their own culture is necessary in this process. Successes and failures outside of the realm of the home provide experiences that strengthen skills needed for survival away from the family.

In addition, relationships with peers offer opportunities for give and take with equals and a chance to learn social skills not possible in the family. Peers do not have the biases and agendas that family members do. An adolescent can receive feedback from peers that is free of the complex issues inherent in family dynamics and family roles. Peers offer a valued perspective.

In peer groups adolescents have a chance to experiment with relationships and learn to deal with rejection as well as acceptance. Also, they learn to resolve conflict and solve problems. They encourage and confront one another, and as their ability to communicate increases, they enjoy participating, competing and cooperating in activities together.

Research on Peers

An ingenious study conducted by Mihaly Csikszentmihalyi and Reed Larson, and described in their book, *Being Adolescent: Conflict and Growth in the Teenage Years* (1984), examines how adolescents spend their time, with whom, and how they feel about it. In order to arrive at a composite picture of the day-to-day lives of average American teenagers, they "followed" a random sample of 75 students chosen from a high school in a community with a heterogeneous population, a mixture of urban and suburban life-styles, and a range of socioeconomic classes and ethnic groups.

The adolescents selected for the study were asked to carry an electronic pager and a pad of paper with them for one week. They were then "beeped" at 50 randomly chosen times during that week. At these times they were asked to record where they were, what they were doing and who they were with. They were also asked to describe their emotional state at the time. Each adolescent was "beeped" from 40 to 50 times.

The results of this study show that as adolescents move from the freshman to the sophomore year, there is an increase in the amount of time adolescents spend with peers. Interestingly, however, this expansion of time does not mean intensification of peer pressure. As a matter of fact, this study reports that as young people mature they exhibit greater freedom from peer influences, with seniors expressing significantly greater independence of thought than freshmen do.

Also, it appears from this study that older adolescents are more comfortable with being alone than younger adolescents are. With age and experience, they stop seeing time by themselves as a probable sign that they are being rejected or avoided. Instead, they may find this time as an opportunity to do interesting things or as a chance for reflection or introspection.

For these reasons, the quality of time adolescents spend with companions and friends is usually enhanced as they get older. With the diminishment of the importance of peer influences, there is less tension and pressure on relationships. When the adolescent does not feel driven to be with peers primarily as a way to feel accepted and assuage insecurities, the peer group becomes a resource for enjoyment, stimulation and expansion of ideas.

The results of this study also show that adolescents express more positive emotional responses while with peers than at any other time. There is a definite preference for being with peers. Adolescents express twice as many negative thoughts while with their family than they do with peers. Since it appears that adolescents feel better with their peers than they do at any other time, these relationships are powerful motivators.

Even though, as this research shows, adolescents clearly prefer being with one another to being with anyone else, and there is no doubt that they enjoy that time tremendously, there is some evidence that there may be some negative effects from too much time with peers. The same researchers found that there is a negative correlation between amount of time spent with friends and school performance and a positive one between time with friends and number of school absences. Also, they found a positive correlation between time with friends and wide mood swings. These correlations were exactly the opposite when time with family was examined. That is, adolescents who spend more time with their families than other adolescents do, perform better in school, have better attendance records and report less moodiness. Time with family appears to add stability to their lives. These researchers conclude that too much socialization is left up to peer groups and that adolescents need positive adult role models including people both inside and outside of the family.

Peers offer much that is valuable, but contact with involved adults is important in the longer-term picture. Adolescents learn from adults by observing them, interacting with them and imitating them. Ideally, an adolescent's life would balance time with peers and time with competent and nurturing adults. It appears that the problem may not be too much time with peers but, instead, not enough time with involved adults.

Peers and Drugs

In summarizing research on peer and family influences on drug use by adolescents, Thomas Glynn (1981) concludes that adolescent drug-using behavior is, at any given time, influenced by both family and peers. There does not appear to be any point where the young person is wholly influenced by one or the other. These influences are not always equal, however, and there are situations where the balance shifts more in one direction than the other.

Adolescents rely on peers and family as resources at different times and under different circumstances. Acceptance of one at a specific time does not mean rejection of the values and influence of the other. For example, an adolescent may experiment with marijuana with peers out of curiosity. (It has been noted that peer influence is particularly strong in initiation to marijuana use.) He or she may decide to use this drug with friends in order to "make a good time better" or to deal with self-consciousness in the group.

This same adolescent may decide to stop using marijuana due to health concerns or because of fear of negative effects. In fact, these are the reasons most commonly mentioned by adolescents for their decision to stop using drugs (Jalali et al., 1981). In this case, family influences would positively predispose the adolescent toward healthy behavior.

On the other hand, this adolescent may develop more serious drug problems if there are stressors within the family. These stressors might include parental alcoholism, workaholism, or illness or marital conflict. It has been noted that when parents abdicate their role, for whatever reason, peer influence will tend to prevail (Sheppard et al., 1985). When this happens, adolescents who have been associating with a drug-using peer group may be more strongly influenced by that group. Other adolescents not previously in such a group may choose a drug-using peer group, because it provides an opportunity to use drugs in order to escape the stressful situation in the family.

Glynn (1981) concludes that when the goal of the drug use is immediate gratification of curiosity or experimentation, peer influence is primary. When drugs are used to deal with underlying psychological or emotional problems, there are usually identifiable family factors involved. Also, it has been suggested that many adolescents who move to the use of illicit drugs other than marijuana are those who have difficulty developing intimate and meaningful ties with their peers. In cases where drug use has become a serious problem, there is often an interactive negative effect from both family and peer influences.

Adolescents need peer groups. However, when there is too much peer involvement, the socialization of the group may supersede parental influence and there is a potential for drug use to become a problem. The answer, of course, is not isolating young people. Those who have problems with peer relationships are also candidates for drug problems. Working out problems with peers is crucial. When this does not happen, the result can be detrimental.

Balance With Other Influences

We have seen that peer groups serve many valuable purposes in the lives of adolescents. Balance is important, however, and these groups, although of primary importance to the adolescent, represent only one aspect of a young person's life. It is important to consider this when addressing the question of why adolescents use drugs.

As indicated in the beginning of this chapter, parents often see their adolescent's association with drug-using peers as the direct cause of that adolescent's drug problem. That is, they believe that these peers created a situation which encouraged their child to use drugs, and that without that situation there would be no problem. While, as we have seen, this view may be partly true, it is oversimplified. The drug-using adolescent may have been attracted to a particular peer group precisely because of the drug use. In some cases adolescents experiment with drugs, like the effect and for any number of reasons (discussed in Chapters One and Two) choose to use drugs more regularly. As part of this choice, young people often select a peer group where drug use is accepted, if not encouraged, and where drugs are available. It is true that groups choose individuals, but individuals also choose groups.

When parents and other adults place all of the blame for adolescent drug problems on peer pressure, they are, in some ways, enabling. That is, they are taking personal responsibility away from the individual adolescent and are implying that this young person had very little choice in the matter. This view encourages dependence and does not help the adolescent begin to be responsible for his or her behavior or the consequences of that behavior. Blaming peers alone does not encourage maturity, because it portrays the adolescent as a reactor rather than an initiator.

While parents need to affirm personal responsibility on the part of the adolescent, they must also remain involved in the young person's life. This may seem to be a contradiction, but it is a reflection of the paradoxical situations parents frequently find themselves in.

To clarify this, it helps to differentiate goals (the ideal) from actual behavior (the real). Parents want adolescents to be independent human beings capable of making responsible decisions. It is important that they treat young people in ways that foster this. This includes expecting the adolescent to accept the consequences of irresponsible behavior. However, the reality is that adolescents have not yet reached full independence and parents are responsible for them. Because of this it is often necessary for parents to structure situations, especially where specific problems have been identified. For example, with adolescents who have identified drug problems, parents may need to require, and monitor, no association with drug-using peers.

Because peers are so important and influential in the lives of adolescents, most programs that treat alcohol and drug problems include a strong peer group component in both inpatient and outpatient programs as well as in aftercare planning (see Chapter Seven). Intervention programs within schools also utilize peers in their programming. (This is discussed in more detail in Chapter Five.)

SOCIETY

While peer influences are clearly important, we cannot overlook the societal context in which they take place. Cultural influences are powerful, especially where young people are concerned. Adolescents today receive messages from a culture which values the immediate gratification of needs, instant cures, and seemingly magical solutions to complex problems. The media provides "proof" that there are simple answers to difficult situations. Advertising tells us that there are a variety of products that will enhance friendship or improve a romance, and one can attain an image of sophistication and maturity through the use of cigarettes or alcohol. It is not surprising that there are so many young people who use drugs to self-medicate when faced with the inevitable stressors of adolescence. Such behavior has been normalized by this culture.

The Acceptance of Drug Taking

Ours is a drug-taking culture, and the effect of this pill-popping mentality is felt by some of us even before birth. The placenta, once considered a protective barrier between mother and fetus, is now recognized to be a semipermeable membrane. Drugs administered to pregnant women quickly enter the fetal bloodstream and interact with the developing neurological system of the fetus. We know that this interaction is potentially dangerous. This is particularly disturbing given that virtually no drug has been proven to be completely safe for the unborn child. Also, some drugs given to mothers during labor stay in the infant's system following birth, sometimes for as long as ten days (Haire, 1978).

People commonly accept that women who abuse alcohol and/or other drugs during their pregnancies greatly risk harming their unborn babies. They find it more difficult to accept the possibility that harm may also be done by established medical practitioners prescribing legal medications.

We are a society accustomed to unquestioningly agreeing to the widespread use of prescribed drugs. Because of this, we are only temporarily shaken by news suggesting that we have been condoning a practice that may need some examining. For example, it has recently been publicized that women who were prescribed DES (diethylstilbestrol) to prevent miscarriages while pregnant, mainly during the 1950s and 1960s, have children who now appear to be suffering subsequent negative effects, including cancer and birth defects. Incidents such as these remind us that approved drugs are not necessarily safe drugs.

Even though we may recognize the risks involved in taking any drug, whether it be prescribed, over-the-counter, or illicit, we are nonetheless subject to a medical system that relies on alleviating pain and discomfort primarily through the use of medication. The basis for this approach is ingrained in our society and is slow to change. As a culture, we frequently do not consider the possible long-term detrimental effects of our actions. We often choose to ignore them when we have the opportunity for quick and dramatic "cures."

There is no question that certain prescribed drugs are essential and lifesaving. Their use is, and should be, accepted procedure. Unfortunately, this acceptance is, in many cases, generalized to situations where the use of drugs may be questionable or dangerous. The risks are often denied. "Taking a pill" is now frequently seen as a remedy for anxiety and sadness, or as relief from boredom or alienation. These are rarely life-endangering situations.

We are a culture where there are more than one billion prescriptions filled each year at a cost of approximately $11.3 billion. It has been estimated that at least one out of eight of these prescriptions is for a drug that is unnecessary, ineffective or actually harmful. In 1978 there were 68 million prescriptions written for minor tranquilizers, and in the same year there were 22,000 admissions to emergency rooms because of tranquilizer misuse (Pizer, 1982).

Doctors continue to prescribe tranquilizers even though it is known that use of these medications may cover emotional problems that could be beneficially treated in other ways. It has been estimated that between 50 and 70 percent of all physical complaints which bring people to seek medical help are of emotional, social or spiritual origin (Rossman, 1982). The treatment for these complaints is often a prescription not for psychotherapy but for a pill.

It should be pointed out that there has been some reaction to our society's widespread use of prescribed and over-the-counter drugs. Even some members of the established medical community have advocated alternatives, though this movement in medical circles is relatively recent. Also, there is a growing number of people who espouse "natural" holistic approaches to healing which are completely separate from traditional medicine.

Ironically, many of these advocates inadvertently perpetuate the very attitudes they protest. For example, emphasizing the use of herbal medication or megadose vitamins as proper treatment for certain symptoms reinforces a belief long held by the established medical community. The belief is that the most effective relief from physical dysfunction or discomfort can be achieved through the introduction of an external substance into the system (the human body).

There are many holistic practices that focus on the utilization of internal resources and processes to enhance healing. These include methods such as biofeedback, imagery, meditation, relaxation, and visualization. They offer true alternatives to a culture that looks to drugs as cures. Practices that emphasize the ingestion of substances, even if these substances are labeled "natural," do not.

Hank Pizer in his *Guide to the New Medicine* (1982) comments, "We seem to have lost faith in our own bodily fortitude and in the idea that in the normal process of living the body heals itself of most ailments" (p. 112).

Adolescents can learn alternative ways to deal with both physical and psychological stress. They can benefit from adult models who respect themselves and their own internal resources. Unfortunately, such models appear to be rare. Malcolm C. Todd (1985), past president of the American Medical Association, has noted: "Much counterproductive and dangerous health behavior is created and sustained by our society's values. Overwork, overeating, self-medication, cigarette smoking, alcohol abuse, the lack of exercise, all are examples" (pp. 10-11).

The Glamor of Drug Taking

Drug taking is frequently portrayed as a glamorous and sophisticated activity to our young people, even though those in the media often deny that this is their intention. Drinking and drug use are depicted many times as exciting and dangerous, thereby indirectly provoking adolescent curiosity.

There are presently many societal forces, including the federal government, working to change this apparent glorification of drugs. This is a complicated task. Some efforts made toward deterring drug use may actually, though not purposefully, encourage it. For example, when adolescents are informed of the possible effects of the use of various drugs, this can, in some instances, arouse interest and provoke experimentation.

Adolescents are concerned primarily with a time frame which focuses on the present and often do not embrace a future-oriented perspective. Also, they are generally risk takers, since they do not acknowledge their own vulnerability. Because of these developmental realities, they will not necessarily use educational information about drugs in the same way adults do. Educational programs need to be designed to take this into account (see Chapters Two and Five).

When a famous actor or musician or well-known sports figure is hospitalized or dies because of a drug overdose, many parents hope that this event will serve as a lesson to their children. In some cases, this may happen. However, the reaction of the young person may sometimes be the opposite of what parents want or expect.

Adolescents tend to romanticize tragic events. Many stars are adulated by young people more after death than they were before. The death provides a situation where the star can be idealized and flaws in character can be ignored or excused. If drug use is involved, adolescents may see it quite differently than their parents do. While parents see the drug use as destructive behavior, the adolescent often creates a scenario where drug use is understandable. The death is seen as the result of an unfortunate circumstance in which the person who died is portrayed as the victim of a "screwed-up" society.

For example, a young man was observed wearing a black t-shirt, listing in clouds the names of Janis Joplin and other rock stars who had died from drug overdoses. The shirt read, "If this is heaven, my time is now." Clearly, wearing this shirt reflected an idolization of these dead stars and an aspiration to be like them. Death was inconsequential.

Parents want adolescents to see that the person's death was that person's responsibility because of his or her own decision to use drugs. Adolescents create an entirely different picture. This picture allows them to identify with what they imagine has happened. As they see it, the person was a victim and, in many ways, so are they.

Also, adolescents will tend to see such a death as an accident that cannot possibly happen to them. They believe that they know how to use drugs safely. This attitude will not necessarily be changed by a dramatic news story. In fact, the story may only serve to make them more determined to prove "It can't happen to me."

CHAPTER FIVE

THE SCHOOLS: IMPLEMENTING
PROGRAMS TO ADDRESS THE PROBLEM

For the first time in this survey's 18-year history, the U.S. public has identified drug use by students as the most important problem facing the public schools.

(Gallup, 1986)

JAN HAWKINS teaches sophomore English at a large suburban high school. Recently, she had noticed some significant changes in behavior on the part of one of her favorite students, Kathy Phillips. Kathy had begun to arrive for class consistently late, and it was clear that during class Kathy was not concentrating. Also, she had been absent on three out of four Mondays. Since Kathy is in Jan's class which is held right after lunch, Jan had been attributing her tardiness to socializing during lunch period and her lack of attention to preoccupation with a new boyfriend. Remembering her own adolescence which involved some weekend "partying," Jan had been looking the other way in regard to the Monday absences and had told herself that Kathy would eventually adjust.

Unfortunately, this has not happened and Kathy's behavior has deteriorated. She has stopped turning in assignments. Her absences, some of them unexcused, have increased. Jan has had to confront the possibility that something more serious is probably occurring, and she has begun to suspect the influence of drugs. Jan sees herself as a teacher, not a counselor, and she is wondering what she should do, since Kathy's behavior is definitely affecting her academic performance.

This scenario is a common one in our schools today. Many people, like Jan, struggle with the problem on their own. Other teachers are fortunate enough to be in schools where people have organized to address the problem. These schools have active student assistance programs, because teachers and administrators have recognized that alcohol and drug abuse interfere with the teaching and learning that should be going on in schools.

If Jan's school had such a program, she would begin by using a checklist (see Appendix A) provided by the student assistance program team. She would then consult with them about the next step to take. This program would be organized in a way that would effectively respond to this need. This chapter explains how such a program can be started and implemented.

WHY THE SCHOOL?

It is commonly accepted by those in the field of substance abuse that the most effective place to intervene and stop drug- or alcohol-abusing behavior is the environment where the abusing person spends the most time. In addition, it is believed that the earlier the intervention occurs, the greater the likelihood that the intervention will be successful, causing the chemically dependent person to enter treatment or to stop using alcohol or drugs altogether. Also, the availability of documented evaluative information about the individual's behavior provides the very essence of a powerful and effective intervention.

Interventions can serve to convince a person that treatment is needed. They can also serve as an influential mirror for individuals regarding their behavior and the consequences attached to that behavior. For adolescents, the earlier this intervention occurs, the greater the potential for adolescents to change their behavior and stop the course of their progression to chemical dependency. On the other hand, interventions which reveal the inability of individuals to make changes and control their substance abuse provide an indication of possible chemical dependence. Interventions and their results can be important data in actual assessments. For example, they can help with the assessment of whether an adolescent is abusing alcohol or drugs and is still somewhat in control, or is actually dependent on alcohol or drugs and has lost control. One way this can be determined is to look at the way in which an adolescent responds to confrontation. When no behavior change occurs, this can be an important indicator of a serious problem.

The school is the most appropriate setting for an early intervention and assessment program aimed at adolescents. Students are accessible at school. Most adolescents spend the greatest amount of their waking hours at school. Since schools maintain records of performance, their structure more easily provides the framework against which to measure behavior and academic achievement over time. The rules and regulations within the school also provide standards against which to measure the acceptability or unacceptability of student behavior. Appropriate interventions can occur at the earliest point possible when significant declines in areas such as achievement and attendance are noted by school personnel.

Schools are in the business of educating. For many, this is a singular goal, and confusion and controversy develop within the school setting when there is movement to deal with any of the psychological issues affecting a student's life. Frequently, there is discomfort in dealing with the personal problems of students, because teachers often view such a focus as outside of their roles as educators. This chapter is designed to provide a workable rationale for the school's involvement in alcohol and drug assessment and intervention.

Schools can benefit through intervention when the behavior of drug taking is affecting the student's ability to learn or the teacher's ability to teach (Anderson, 1981). Students who are using drugs or alcohol throughout the day present numerous barriers to teaching. The student who has smoked marijuana before class sleeps through the class. The student who cannot seem to remain focused on the material presented in class is frequently a student who is involved in alcohol or drug using. Students who have been drinking often become involved in fights. Students can also become involved in a world and culture which focuses on drugs and alcohol. As this world gains in status and importance, students' academic motivation decreases, as does their performance and sense of direction.

Also, the students who are concerned about parental drinking problems are often preoccupied with problems at home. This can be overwhelming and can drain the student's productive energy. All of these students present very special teaching problems. Unfortunately, the basic underlying problems are usually not addressed, because school personnel often feel that dealing with these problems is not within their realm of expertise or responsibility. A student assistance program designed to address such problems can help to create a milieu that is conducive to teaching. This program can help teachers to develop skills for responding to behaviors indicating possible problems with drugs. In addition, teachers can be directly assisted in making referrals to the appropriate person for student assessment and intervention. A student assistance program can free the teacher in many ways so that teaching becomes the teacher's primary activity and issues of control become secondary.

This chapter addresses the school's role in dealing with drug and alcohol abuse among students. The student assistance program is discussed and described in terms of its linkage with the community and local treatment providers. It is a guide for program implementation on all levels. Administrators may decide to implement such a program in their school. A community group or task force may take on such a project and therefore provide the impetus for implementation. Treatment centers may work with local schools to develop such a program in the interest of continuity of care and may deal with such aspects as identifying those needing treatment and aftercare planning for those who have had treatment.

THE STUDENT ASSISTANCE PROGRAM

The student assistance program is modeled after the employee assistance programs found in business and industry (Anderson, 1981). The purpose of employee assistance programs is to intervene and assist in the problems of employees in relation to how such problems affect work performance. School-based intervention programs deal with substance abuse problems that impede learning and associated school performance. A philosophy based on a belief in early intervention and support underlies the student assistance program model. The school is also in the position of assuring anonymity with the purpose of reducing the risk of stigmatization among students or harmful labeling among faculty. While the need for such anonymity would seem apparent in the case of the drug- or alcohol-abusing young person, the need for anonymity is as imperative for the adolescent who is the child of an alcoholic parent. In most cases the alcoholic parent is resistant to the involvement of his or her child in such a program, since it can represent a severe threat to the parent's continued drinking. From this parent's perspective, providing services to their child is often viewed as a personal hindrance to drinking rather than helping the child. A student assistance program within the school setting, therefore, provides a safe and anonymous environment for students to receive help with alcohol and drug abuse problems of their own, as well as help for problems that result from parental alcoholism.

Program Tasks

The student assistance program can be described in terms of its functions. First, the program identifies those students in need of services. Such identification is behavioral and performance based. Therefore, identification is based on fact and not rumor, and rationality rather than emotionality. Clearly identifiable is the student who is drinking alcohol in the bathroom, or smoking pot on school grounds, or the student who smells heavily of alcohol after lunch period. Not such obvious signals, but critical ones nonetheless, are signs such as a student who sleeps in class, a student whose attitude in the classroom becomes suddenly negative, or a student whose academic performance declines markedly. The process of documenting such behavioral data underlies early intervention.

A second function of student assistance programs is one of motivation. A program without the ability to influence motivation, without the ability to encourage students to utilize the services offered, is impotent. Such motivation can take various forms, from fostering the desire on the part of the individual student for a healthier life to applying coercive pressure so that a student might accept the recommendations to receive the program services. Such coercive action might involve refusing the student various privileges within the school, even enrollment in the school, unless there is program involvement.

It has been our experience in working with schools where there are active student assistance programs that this approach can be quite effective in helping students. For example, one student assistance program counselor worked with an alcohol-abusing student for two months to encourage him to seek help. Then this student had a serious car accident while under the influence of alcohol, risking both his life and that of his girlfriend. The previous motivational counseling provided a bridge back to the counselor, and the young person began to understand the seriousness of his problem. Together, they worked out plans to talk with his parents and seek professional help.

Another student was caught intoxicated at a school dance. She was given the option of a three-day suspension or involvement in the alcohol and drug awareness group. She chose the group and through the group was able to make some important decisions about drinking. As a result of the group involvement, she changed her behavior and never again showed signs of drinking at school functions.

Student athletes often are required to sign agreements not to use alcohol or drugs. If it is suspected (or known) that a student has been using drugs, he or she may be given a warning and encouraged to participate in the student assistance program by attending chemical awareness groups. If pressure is needed, the student's refusal to cooperate can result in suspension from the team.

In one school, a star athlete was the subject of rumors that he was abusing marijuana. Other team members were reluctant to confront this, but a knowledgeable coach requested his participation in a chemical awareness group. As a result of participation in the group, he admitted the problem and made a commitment to honor the contract.

Organizational Structure

The student assistance program is not a one-person program (see Appendix B). It is organized so that many people in the school bring their energies and resources together to plan and implement the program. Working with chemically involved adolescents can be difficult and demanding work. Team members need support from one another in this process. Team members also need to provide a mirror to one another and to confront one another with regard to enabling behaviors such as overlooking signs of problems in favorite students. The organizational structure of the student assistance program within the school is comprised of an administrator, a core team with a coordinator, and an advisory committee.

The Administrator

The role of the administrator is one of providing sanction to the program and motivation through the authority of his/her role. The administrator is actively involved in the development of policies and procedures that relate not only to the student assistance program but also to drug and alcohol use among students in the school. It is the administrator's belief in the program that sanctions it. It is the administrator's willingness to enforce policies and procedures that will serve to influence students to participate. Many in-school task forces have organized student assistance programs without the support and early involvement of this key person, only to find themselves with an effective-on-paper program but an impotent program in reality. The need for active involvement on this level cannot be overstressed. The administrator not only sanctions the program in terms of clout relative to the enforcement of policies and procedures, but the administrator also sanctions the program financially. The student assistance program requires a budget to be functional as a credible and viable program. In order to provide active support fiscally and administratively, the administrator must generally believe in the program.

We have found that the principal's attitude is a crucial element in effecting the student assistance program. It can be the key to the success or failure of the program.

In one school, the students all seemed to know that the principal did not think drug or alcohol use was a serious issue. Each time the student assistance program team looked to him to provide consequences for in-school alcohol or drug use, he dismissed it as just a little normal fun. As a result, the students did not see the program, or drug and alcohol use, as serious. Adults provide the standards against which young people often measure themselves, and since this administrator did not set high standards in this regard, neither apparently did the students. In this school, the student assistance program was underutilized by both students and teachers, not because a problem did not exist, but because the principal, through his behavior, said it was not important.

The Core Team

The core team is comprised of interested individuals from within the school. The core team is interdisciplinary in nature and seeks to bring a variety of skills together to ensure that all bases are covered both in program planning and implementation. The multidisciplinary aspect also serves to reduce the potential competition and resentment that can arise among school departments when a program is located within a particular department and some faculty members feel left out. Team members need a variety of skills, from record keeping to group facilitation. The tasks of the team include maintaining in-school public relations and community public relations, conducting student assessment, facilitating support groups, providing referrals and developing policies and procedures.

The core team is comprised of the workers who carry out the program. These are the people whose energy, ideas and commitment make up the program. The team is led by the coordinator, who, for most schools, will require that a minimum of half of his/her time will be devoted to the student assistance program. This is important, since there are so many responsibilities. The coordinator should be skilled in all functions of the program and should be able to conduct assessments, lead groups, conduct public relations activities and record program statistics. As the title implies, this person coordinates the entire program by linking its components. A minimum of one member representing supportive services such as social work, psychology or guidance should be on the team. The team should also include the school nurse and interested teachers. As indicated earlier, the team members are the workers of the program. Team members serve as contact persons for students and thereby are an accessible link to the program. They can also serve as group facilitators or provide the internal public relations for the program. Individual team members do not provide all of these services but only the ones they are skilled at. Team members should not be overloaded, as they have other responsibilities within the school. Whenever possible, administrators are encouraged to provide release time for core team members.

It is sometimes desirable to rotate team members on a regular basis in order to avoid burnout and to encourage broad faculty involvement. Working with alcohol- and substance-abusing adolescents can be draining and demanding. A rotation of active team members assures continued energy in the program. Planning rotations so that team members get a semester or year-long break every few years helps tremendously.

This rotation should be planned so that there are always some experienced members remaining to assist the newer ones. Also, rotation should not occur so rapidly that individual training and experience are not fully utilized.

It is also helpful if team members can be involved with a professional support group comprised of members of student assistance personnel from programs in other schools. This group provides a forum for team members to talk about the difficult job of working with adolescents with these problems. Also, members gain support in their efforts to continue to effectively carry out a challenging task.

The Advisory Committee

The advisory committee provides guidance for the core team and administrator. The advisory committee is comprised of community individuals who can bring direction to the program. These skills will include expertise in such areas as alcohol and other drug abuse, counseling, adolescence, and children of alcoholics issues. As the core team is beginning to address the problem of alcohol and drug abuse in the school, the guidance of a committee of experts in programming and delivering services is critical. The advisory committee should also include someone from the local police department, since these people are in the position of enforcing laws related to the use of alcohol and other drugs on school grounds, as well as in the community. A person from the juvenile justice system might be helpful in bringing a new perspective to working with youth. This person could also provide additional clout for utilization of school student assistance programs for students who are already involved in the judicial system. The court system could then refer directly to a school program. It would be wise to include one or two parents to ensure that support is forthcoming from a group such as the parent-teacher association and to act as a liaison to other parents in the school. A student who has successfully completed treatment for drug problems would add an important additional dimension as a representative on the advisory committee. Finally, it is recommended that the community be represented. This involvement can be achieved through the inclusion of a member of the community service agencies such as the Kiwanis Club or the Junior League. These groups can serve not only as a liaison to the community but can also be a source of funding. The community advisory committee members, then, are chosen according to their ability to advise in addition to their ability to provide support to the program.

Philosophy, Policies and Procedures

The philosophy, policies and procedures give guidance, direction and purpose to an effective student assistance program (see Appendices C and D). Their development is a critical element in student assistance programs. Without them a program has little direction, and personnel will feel as if they are managing one crisis after another without having significant impact on any one student. Schools that operate student assistance programs without well thought out and consistent philosophies, policies and procedures run the risk of high staff burnout and student apathy.

A philosophy statement (Appendix C) clarifies the beliefs and values that govern thought and conduct. The philosophy statement outlines a set of principles that set the program in motion and give it direction. The philosophy statement describes what the school believes to be true about students and alcohol and drug use and abuse. Additionally, it addresses the school's role and responsibilities with respect to these problems.

The school policy (Appendix D) is the statement of the plan or course of action. The policy statement discusses the manner in which the school will respond to various situations involving drug and alcohol use and abuse. It also describes the procedures, which are the actual courses of action to be taken including how and when students will become involved in the student assistance program. Procedures include step-by-step descriptions of the process. Procedures address the specifics and are developed with consideration given to internal school rules and public laws.

The philosophy, policies and procedures relate not only to the student assistance program but also to the larger school organization. These statements direct all action regarding any student's alcohol or drug use. In each case of student drug or alcohol abuse, the policy statement should describe a specific course of action including contingencies for repeat offenses.

The philosophy, policies and procedures are best developed with the involvement of the entire student assistance program organizational membership. All members of the organizational membership have important contributions to make to the development of the philosophy. It is important for the administrator to be involved at this level. If this person is not involved in the development of the philosophy statement, it is unlikely that policies and procedures will be carried out. Additionally, it is helpful to involve advisory committee members in the creation of the philosophy statement, as they represent groups which are critical to program success. Subsequently, the policies and procedures can be developed by the administrator and the core team, since these people are in the position to interpret the philosophy through actual practice.

Training and In-Service

Once the organizational structure is established and team members have been chosen, it is imperative that this group of people receive training in the area of alcohol and other drug abuse. It is not enough to assume that these people know all they need to know simply because they have identified student alcohol and drug abuse as a problem in their school. They require training regarding substance abuse and adolescent development, the progression, the denial system, chemical dependency and the family, and intervention. Training also needs to include initiation, implementation and evaluation of the student assistance program, as well as the development of a philosophy statement and a policy statement describing procedures to be carried out. Team members will need training in the area of in-school assessment, the in-school intervention, and group process skills.

In developing and conducting this training and in-service program, it is wise to be aware that training in the area of chemical dependency frequently serves to bring to the surface powerful issues for the participants. It is not uncommon for participants to examine their own drinking practices or for those participants to come to an awareness that a family member is an alcoholic. Professional trainers must be sensitive to these issues and equipped to deal with them. It is also helpful for core team members to be aware of the possibility of recognizing personal concerns so that they can be prepared for the intensity of the training.

It has been our experience that the recognition of alcohol or drug problems in a team member's family occurs frequently during training. For example, a teacher who participated in the group training we provided for the core team at her school had a significant raising of her awareness about this issue. This teacher had elected to participate because she had been teaching history for ten years and was looking for a new challenge. Also, she had been concerned about the increase in drug use among students at her school. Through her active involvement in the training, she realized her own husband was an alcoholic. She shared this with the professionals providing the training, and they were able to make an appropriate referral which resulted in involvement in treatment programs for both the teacher and her husband.

The following outlines are suggested agendas for training. Each session can run from two to six hours.

Adolescents and Chemical Dependency

Objectives

1. Participants will be able to define various terms as they relate to adolescent chemical dependency.
2. Participants will understand the concept of enabling as it relates to their role in the school setting.
3. Participants will understand the motivation for initial chemical experimentation along with the motivation for sustained use.
4. Participants will understand the consequences of alcohol use from the perspective of the adolescent, the school, the family and the community.
5. Participants will develop an orientation to the treatment of chemical dependency.

6. Participants will understand the chemically dependent family system.

Session One: The Chemically Dependent Adolescent

Etiology
Definition of terms
    Chemical dependency
    Stages of alcohol and drug use progression
    The denial system
    Enabling
Adolescent development and chemical dependency
Families of chemically dependent adolescents
Adolescent treatment
    Phases of recovery
    Aftercare issues
    Treatment philosophies
    Treatment modalities

Session Two: The Chemically Dependent Family

The concept of family systems theory
The family illness; family roles
The adolescent co-dependent; special needs
Intervention; breaking through denial:
    With the chemically dependent adult
    With the chemically dependent adolescent

Student Assistance Programs, Helping Students With Drug and Alcohol Problems

This training should follow the previously described session, so that participants have had introductory training in the area of adolescent and chemical dependency.

Objectives

1. Participants will understand the structure and function of the student assistance program.
2. Participants will understand the role schools play in enabling.
3. Participants will develop skills in in-school assessment and intervention.

Session One: The Student Assistance Program

Organizational structure of the student assistance program
Program goals and tasks
Philosophy and policy and procedure development
Schools and enabling

Session Two: Program Implementation

Identification, assessment and intervention in the school setting
Program services
    In-school Assessment Skill Building
    Chemical Awareness Group
    Aftercare Support Group
    Concerned Persons Group

Assessment and Intervention in the School Setting: Skill Building

This is primarily a skill-building workshop and should follow the adolescent chemical-dependency workshop and the student assistance workshops. The focus during this workshop is on practice rather than on lecture, providing participants with not only theoretical information but with practical skills.

Objectives

1. Participants will understand that assessment is a process, not simply an event.
2. Participants will develop skill in defining behaviors that are indicators of alcohol and drug using.
3. Participants will develop skills in working with these problem behaviors.
4. Participants will develop skills in conducting an assessment interview and utilizing assessment tools.
5. Participants will develop skills in linking problems with drug and alcohol abusing.

Session One: Assessment Theory

Assessment as process rather than event
Reducing enabling as part of assessment
Groups as assessment forums
Assessment tools

Session Two: Assessment Practicum

 The assessment interview
 The assessment and intervention process
 The role of confrontation in intervention

Follow-Up

Once the core team has been trained, has developed the program philosophy, and a policy and procedure statement, and has developed a program outlining which students will be served and how the team is to provide in-service training to the general faculty and the students, two separate in-services are recommended: one for the faculty and one for the students. This will allow the in-service program to focus on the benefits specific to each group. It is this type of focus that will ensure acceptance of the program and participation by students and faculty in the program. Students need to see the program as something they can trust, not as a "search-and-destroy" program. Teachers need to view the program as something that will ultimately assist them in doing a better job of teaching. These in-service training sessions can be short, each ranging from a one- to three-hour program. The goal in each should be a description of services to be provided, with an emphasis on the benefits of the program.

Teacher In-Service

 Use, abuse and dependency among adolescents
 Alcohol and drug abuse; academic and behavioral problems among
    students
 How the student assistance program works
    Services offered
    Referral mechanism
    The role of the classroom teacher
 Introduction of student assistance program personnel

Student In-Service

 How the student assistance program works
 Who can use the program
 How do students get into the program
 Introduction of student assistance program personnel

Teacher in-services can be conducted at a faculty meeting. It is important to provide education concerning adolescent student substance abuse and chemical dependency in addition to describing the program. Since it is possible that this program could be seen as "just another program" and more work, student assistance program personnel are wise to offer it as a program that frees teacher time to educate as well as to effectively deal with the drug and alcohol problems presented in the classroom. Thus, the student assistance program reduces and resolves such problems in the classroom.

Presentations to students are most effective when conducted in small groups such as in homeroom classes. Results are most effectively achieved with students through a focus on confidentiality, trust and what the program can do for students as individuals. The goal during this presentation is to enhance the willingness of students to use the program. It is helpful to clearly explain the program policy and procedure in regard to confidentiality. Students are more likely to participate in a program when explanations are clear.

Initially, ongoing inservice is required to maintain this program. The faculty will require continual updating which will also serve to encourage continued program participation. It should be noted, though, that as the student assistance program becomes a more established part of the school network, it would be expected that there would be a decreased need for continual in-service.

As the program becomes accepted in a school, the nature of referral systems does as well. For example, we interviewed one student assistance program counselor who reported that initially she had to develop ways to get students into her group. Additionally, in the early days of her program, she found most of the referrals coming from the faculty. However, after a number of years, the program had developed a good reputation and the program no longer had to seek referrals. The majority of referrals came from students themselves. The program worked and the students knew it.

The Program in Action

The main purpose of the student assistance program is to address student academic needs as they are affected by alcohol and/or drug problems. There are generally three primary groups served by these programs. These are:

Alcohol/Drug Abusers

Students whose own use of alcohol and other drugs appears to be problematic require intervention in such cases at an early point in time which can interrupt the pattern of destructive usage. Groups for these students are called "chemical awareness groups."

Chemically Dependent Adolescents

Students who are diagnosed as chemically dependent and are returning from treatment programs frequently find their peers in school to be a threat to their sobriety. For many recovering adolescents, school is a place to be feared, as it is viewed as being comprised of other students who use drugs. Contact with old using friends provides difficult challenges many young people do not feel ready to meet. Those students are in need of services supportive of their drug-free life-style. Groups for these students are called "aftercare support groups."

Affected Family Members

Students experiencing problems as a result of abusive drinking or drug use on the part of a family member represent a group considered to be at high risk for developing alcoholism themselves. They can be taught to deal with the stresses of an alcoholic home in order to prevent their turning to alcohol and drugs themselves. They can also learn that chemical dependency is a family problem, and they need to be prepared to recognize certain warning signs for themselves. Groups for these students are called "concerned persons groups."

Chemical Awareness Group

Assessment is the process of determining the likelihood that behavioral or academic problems are related to a drug or alcohol problem. A chemical awareness group is an invaluable tool for determining the nature of a young person's substance abuse. This group provides a forum for the students' self-evaluation regarding their drug and alcohol use. The group is comprised of peers who work together to make decisions about their use. The group is organized to provide education, values clarification, decision making, peer support and confrontation. The end result of this group is that students will not only make decisions about their chemical use, but that the group will also have effected a change in how individuals see the role of chemical use in their lives, and that these individuals will have made changes based on their new views. Additionally, an individual assessment can occur. This is a formal process of gathering data from the student and those significant others to determine the severity of use and the effect the use has had on the young person's life.

The chemical awareness group is undoubtedly the most difficult group to begin. Students in need of assessment are frequently the last to be aware of the need. Denial is strong and is accompanied by resistance. Given a student-focused presentation of the program, it is possible to attract students who have an awareness of their problems and are willing to discuss them. However, a number of students being referred into this program can come through the various disciplinary procedures within the school. The vice-principal is encouraged to make referrals in cases of in-school use or possession. Faculty are encouraged to make referrals when they suspect that a decline in academic performance or behavioral problems are related to drugs or alcohol. Core team members discuss these students with faculty. Acting as advisors, core members regularly ask the question, "Could this be an alcohol or drug problem?" As faculty members make referrals and experience success, the likelihood of additional referrals will increase.

Intervention and the Group as Part of Assessment

Assessment is a process that occurs over time and should not be confused with an assessment interview. While assessment interviews may well be part of the program, this is not where the focus should be placed. If the assessment is viewed as a process that connects interventions and the response to these interventions, then the determination regarding the likelihood of a serious alcohol or drug problem will seem clear. For each observation of an inappropriate behavior or a change in behavior that represents dysfunction, a student should receive a response from someone within the school. It is the student's response to this action that begins the process of determining whether there is indication of a serious drug or alcohol problem. Chemically dependent adolescents are not in control of their behavior and, therefore, cannot change behavior in response to interventions. There is a much greater likelihood on the part of the substance abuser, the non-chemically dependent adolescent, to make a change in behavior based on intervention.

For our purposes here, intervention is defined as confronting the student with the inappropriate behavior through a mirroring of that behavior to the student. Essentially, then, a confrontation involves informing the student that the behavior is noted and, if appropriate, providing consequences for the behavior. In this way the student is assisted in becoming accountable for his/her behavior. At this point the student is in a position of needing to make a decision. The decision involves deciding whether continuing the behavior is worth the consequences. Herein lies the key to assessment in determining the likelihood for dependency or a serious drug or alcohol problem. The chemically dependent adolescent, by the nature of his/her disease, is not able to make the decision to no longer use alcohol or other drugs. The chemically dependent adolescent, like an alcoholic adult, is willing to sacrifice much to continue using alcohol or other drugs. Through a regular process of mirroring back the behavior and providing consequences, students are given the chance, in small steps, to change their behavior. These interventions and the student's ability to respond to them become the data-gathering mechanism for the assessment. The following case examples demonstrate how this takes place.

Brian, a high school junior, was referred to Mr. Stevens, a school counselor who was part of the student assessment core team. He was referred because he was sleeping in class after his lunch hour and smelled mildly of alcohol. Before meeting with Brian, Mr. Stevens did some homework of his own. He checked Brian's grades and found a decline since the previous year on his overall average with a remarkable shift from A work to C/D work in his post-lunch hour class. In gathering information from Brian's teachers, Mr. Stevens found that there had been a subtle shift in Brian's attitude, with less participation in class and less enthusiasm for coursework.

In a discussion with Mr. Stevens, Brian stated that he was convinced he did not have a problem with alcohol. Mr. Stevens raised his concerns about a possible connection between Brian's drinking and his grades. Brian was adamant that there was no connection. He explained his lack of enthusiasm by saying that his classes were boring. Mr. Stevens explained to Brian that he was not certain that Brian had a problem but thought that it might be helpful for him to take a little closer look at his alcohol use. He suggested that Brian join the chemical awareness group and Brian agreed.

Through this group Brian learned about alcohol abuse and dependency. The group challenged him not to drink during lunch period for two weeks and at the same time examine the difference that this made in his achievement at school. Brian succeeded in meeting the challenge and liked his classroom performance. He then made a decision to change his use and no longer drank beer with his friends during lunch hour. His grades improved, as did his class participation. Brian was not chemically dependent. Through the group process he was able to make some decisions about his alcohol use, having realized there was a connection between his use and his declining grades.

Claire, on the other hand, had been through the chemical awareness group the previous year. Mr. Stevens had felt optimistic about her ability to progress but wondered how serious her problem might be. She seemed to improve academically during the time she was in the group, but after leaving the group her grades declined. Claire made numerous promises to Mr. Stevens to improve. Each of these promises was broken. She began to avoid him when she saw him in the halls and was frequently truant. On the first day of the new school year she was caught with marijuana in the bathroom. The police were called. Her parents were informed and so was Mr. Stevens. Claire was released to her parents. Mr. Stevens and Claire's parents discussed the problem at length. Claire refused to participate in any treatment program.

One month later, Claire was arrested for shoplifting. The judge, with input from her parents and Mr. Stevens, made participation in a treatment program a condition of Claire's probation. Claire's recovery was difficult, but she completed an inpatient treatment program and returned to the aftercare support group in the school. Claire was indeed chemically dependent. Faced with repeated consequences for her behavior, over time she was unable to change without significant pressure. However, this pressure resulted in successful treatment.

It is important to emphasize the value of this assessment being viewed as a process. Unlike an assessment interview which is actually somewhat of an academic process, the assessment process is also an intervention process at the same time. Limits and consequences are set in motion as assessment proceeds. Gradually, the forces come to bear on the student; the student determines that there are few options other than to change his/her drug or alcohol using, and if this is not possible the student will have to seek treatment. By the time the student seeks treatment, the student has begun to accept that drug and alcohol use is out of hand and his or her life has become unmanageable. This student is in an ideal place to significantly benefit from treatment. Precious time in treatment is not expended convincing the student that he or she has a problem, because the assessment and intervention process has facilitated readiness for treatment.

It is important that the goal of any assessment or intervention in the school be one of encouraging the student to question personal behavior. This is the purpose of mirroring back the behavior and essentially informing the student of what was observed. In-school assessment is not a "search-and-destroy" mission; its goal is not to obtain incriminating information regarding a student's drug and alcohol usage but rather to facilitate questioning the role alcohol and drugs play in the student's life. An assessment should be viewed as a collaboration, a process of mutual problem solving. Without this type of approach, while specific information may be obtained, it is likely that the student will become hostile and resistant to any help or guidance that may be offered. Information about students is of little value without the ability to use it to help the student. The purpose of an in-school intervention program is to help the student, not simply to obtain information. This is the guiding force behind school programs of this sort.

Format of the Group

Students referred to the chemical awareness group have usually demonstrated some kind of problem with alcohol and drugs. The group is then utilized to provide a forum for assessment over time. Basically, group members are given some education, become involved in personal discussion regarding their use of alcohol or drugs, and are asked to make some sort of commitment regarding changing their behavior. They are monitored, and monitor each other, regarding their ability to actually achieve the change to which they have agreed. It is the students who do not seem able to make any changes who will appear as a high risk for chemical dependency.

This is a structured group. The group should be time limited (10-12 weeks) to emphasize the concept of decision making and change within a specific time frame. Facilitators involved in a group that is open-ended are at risk of enabling because they will not be as likely to push for decision making. The risk is extremely high with this group, as we are discussing a group of students who are using drug and alcohol and who have been experiencing some problems. In a situation such as this, it is helpful for the group structure to provide the boundaries and limits, rather than require that the facilitator set them continuously. The focus, then, is to provide an experience, both educationally and experientially, whereby the student assesses his/her own alcohol- or drug-using behavior. The following represents a sample structure for this assessment group. Each session can be from one to two hours in length, and sessions should take place once a week.

Session One: Orientation

During this first session, the facilitator recognizes that the students referred to this group may have a variety of feelings regarding how they came to be part of this group. The facilitator explains rules, regulations and expectations, and the issue of confidentiality is discussed so that students are informed of where information will go and who has access to it. The facilitator then delineates his or her own boundaries regarding confidentiality according to school policies and procedures. Most facilitators announce that confidentiality will be respected except in cases which are judged to be life-endangering.

The facilitator encourages a discussion of feelings regarding how students came to be in this group. While direct confrontation of a student's denial of a problem is not encouraged at this early date, a subtle process of mirroring back those problem behaviors that resulted in referral can gently initiate the process of breaking through denial. It is critical to form a cooperative relationship with the student at an early point in order to address the denial without alienating students. If the students feel that someone is trying to understand them, even though they may not accept the behavior, students will be more receptive to confrontation and will be more likely to consider changing.

Session Two: The Progression

During this session, the progression of drug and alcohol use, from experimentation to complete dependency, is discussed. The approach here is not one of using scare tactics but of providing factual information. The progression should not be presented in a way that indicates that anyone who experiments will become chemically dependent. Students are, however, helped in understanding that there are risks associated with increased use. The further along the progression that people move, the greater the difficulty in reversing the course and the greater the number of life problems associated with use. After a discussion of the progression, the life history exercise can be instrumental in helping students transfer the progression to their own life experience. In this exercise, students are instructed to draw a horizontal line on a piece of paper. The far left-hand side of the line represents birth and the far right side of the line represents death. Students are instructed to draw a line representing their current age. At this point students are instructed to note critical events on their life line. These events will include successes and failures and good times and bad times. Sometimes, as students are working on this exercise it is helpful for the facilitator to ask questions which may stimulate the thinking process. This might include such questions as, "What was going on when you were five?" "What are the events of the seventh grade that you remember the most?" "How were your grades in eighth grade?" "Were you involved in sports at any time?"

and "Have you ever been involved in any legal trouble or been expelled from school?" Students are encouraged to include as much data on this time line as possible. Students are instructed to construct another time line. This time line will represent their own progression of drug and alcohol use. On the top of the line they are to note types and amounts of chemicals used and frequency of use. Underneath the time line they are to note feelings while using them and about their use of them. Students are reminded that this exercise is personal and they will share only those details with the group that they choose to share.

The final stage of this exercise is putting the time line and progression line together. Students are to match the life lines up so that the years on each line correspond. The facilitator then asks a series of questions to promote self-assessment and self-awareness regarding the life line. These questions might include:

1. Note the first problem or disappointment you experienced. Now look at your level of drug or alcohol usage. How much and how often were you using?
2. Consider the feelings associated with using. Were they good feelings when they first began? Did it become less fun and something you did simply because you did it?
3. When did you begin to experience family problems? How much were you using at the time?
4. If you continue using, what will your life line look like in one year, two years, five years, ten years?
5. Retain the picture of you in ten years if you continue to use. Does it remind you of anyone in your family who perhaps has a drug or alcohol problem?

Through this exercise students begin to take a personal look at their using. It is helpful at this point to facilitate a group discussion of this exercise by asking if anyone would like to share anything he or she learned. Group members can be asked if they experienced any feelings while they were doing this exercise. Group facilitators should note that this is probably the first time students have considered their drug use in this way. The average alcohol- and/or drug-abusing adolescent lives for today and seldom looks to the future. This exercise provides a chance to change perspective.

Session Three: Personal Assessment

Students complete a questionnaire regarding alcohol and drug abuse (Appendix E). It is most helpful to use a self-scoring questionnaire so students can retain responsibility for the process. Remember that the goal in this group is to facilitate self-awareness on the part of the student, not to obtain information about the student. At this time, it is also helpful to ask students to pair up and verbally administer the questionnaire to each other. This begins the process of working together and provides accountability among students. Students have a good idea of the use of their peers and at this point will hold them accountable for minimizing that use. Again, a group discussion is facilitated, asking group members to discuss what they have learned.

Session Four: Personal Contract

During this session group members are asked to make a commitment to the group to change their pattern of use. A written contract is usually very effective in this type of situation. Additionally, it is effective to pair group members in a "buddy system" to provide support and additional accountability.

Session Five: Defenses and Denial

The defenses used by chemically abusing people to keep from changing are discussed. As each person reports on their contract, denial is discussed and the defenses are related specifically to the success or lack of success of each person in maintaining their contract.

Session Six: The Family

The family is discussed as it relates to substance abuse. It is important here to provide discussion which is general enough to allow for the fact that some of these students may be children of alcoholic parents. Again, group members are asked to report back on their contracts.

Session Seven: Reassessment and Recontracting

Students are asked to report to the group how their contracts are going. They are asked to discuss any problems they have been having, either at school or at home. Other group members are encouraged to respond and to confront reports that are not accurate. Students are then required to agree to contracts again. Based on the results of the first contract, there may be modifications. As always, students who are doing well are supported and encouraged to continue.

Session Eight: Another's Story

A recovering young person is asked to speak to the group about his/

her progression and recovery process. Students are asked to report back to the group regarding the progress on their contracts.

Session Nine: Evaluation

This entire session is spent in self-evaluation and peer evaluation. One student at a time gives a self-evaluation to the group and requests feedback from the group and the facilitator regarding the progress they have made. Students request recommendations regarding what to do from peers and the facilitator. Some students may be referred to a primary treatment program; some may be referred to AA/NA and an aftercare group if they are committed to abstinence. Some may leave the group wishing to make no changes. Some may leave having changed their use and requiring no additional work.

Session Ten: Closure

This session is used for closure to ensure that students are following through on their plans. Ongoing one-to-one contacts may be scheduled with the group facilitator. Students are asked to discuss with each other how this group has made an impact on their lives and discuss the plans they have made to maintain that impact.

Aftercare Support Group

Aftercare services should be provided to young people who are returning from primary inpatient treatment programs and require a supportive network within the school. Aftercare services include a support group for selected students who have completed primary treatment. This group is structured as a support group. The facilitator should not take the role of therapist whose goal is to affect change but rather take the role of a caring professional whose goal is to support the change process that is occurring. It should be noted here that we advocate that all students receiving aftercare services be required to be involved in some kind of continuing treatment program in the community. Primary inpatient treatment is viewed as an intensive beginning to long-term treatment. If a student is not involved in a continuing treatment program, the student assistance program should advocate for such involvement and make the necessary referral to a professional agency prepared to deal with such treatment. If a student is involved in such treatment, the support group should require ongoing involvement and treatment completion as a condition of continued support group involvement.

While the authors recognize the value of Alcoholics Anonymous and Narcotics Anonymous, it is encouraged that the student also be involved in a continuing treatment program staffed and directed by professionals trained to treat chemical dependency. Recovery, as discussed previously, involves a great deal more than attending a school group once a week. Additionally, the average school group facilitator is not as effective at recognizing signs of relapse as a trained professional might be.

Student assistance programs that do not establish such conditions will find themselves in the position of attempting to provide primary services to a young person who has not solidified personal recovery. These school personnel risk enabling, because they are taking inappropriate responsibility for the situation. Young people without continuing treatment programs are most often viewed as "talking the jargon" of a recovery program with little significant integration of the personality and life changes which are necessary for a productive and healthy life.

In addition, young people who are involved in a recovery program receive individual support in the aftercare group. This is provided in two ways. First, the young person establishes a network of peers to contact and receive support from. Additionally, the student assistance program personnel are available to the student to help deal with any in-school crisis that may pose a threat to the student's abstinence.

Starting the Group

The aftercare support group is a relatively simple group to begin. However, difficulty sometimes arises in identifying those students who are returning from treatment programs. In spite of the movement to reduce the stigma attached with drug and alcohol treatment, many individuals are not comfortable with their treatment becoming public knowledge. It is not unusual for a student to return from an inpatient treatment program without informing the school. The core team will need to do some organizing and networking in the community to deal with this problem.

Core team members are advised to contact the area treatment centers and explain the in-school support program that is being offered. They should encourage the treatment center to develop policies and procedures that involve communicating with the student's school, and request that the treatment center inform the school, with the student's informed consent, when a student enters treatment. It is also important to inform the treatment center that the school would like to be involved in staff meetings and in discharge planning for students. Treatment centers can be encouraged to make referrals to in-school support group programs a part of their normal discharge recommendations. Schools are encouraged to take responsibility for re-entry planning. Treatment centers and schools can and should work together for the recovery of each student. Through a sound liaison with treatment centers, referrals to the aftercare support group can become automatic.

Structure of the Group

The structure of the aftercare group is organized around discussing obstacles to recovery. This involves support from the group for positive steps toward recovery and confrontation from the group for behaviors that might appear to endanger recovery. The group is not structured with an agenda as are some of the other school support groups but, rather, is planned to allow each person an opportunity to report on how things are going for him or her and to let the group know if he or she needs time to discuss some specific problem areas or difficulties with recovery. This group should meet once or twice a week, and members should participate in the group for as long as they need to. Sessions can be from one to two hours in length.

Concerned Persons Group

Services should be provided to children of chemically dependent parents. Research indicates that this group of children is greatly at risk in terms of developing chemical dependency themselves. For this reason, the provision of support group services to this population of students can be viewed not only as intervention but probably more accurately as prevention. The support group for these students is designed to provide some basic education about alcoholism in the family. Students discuss the issues related to living in an alcoholic family. These issues include such things as how to deal with the stresses of an alcoholic home and learning about their own vulnerability to the use of drugs and alcohol as a coping mechanism. As there appears to be a high correlation between child abuse and alcoholism, self-protection is an important issue. It is extremely important to provide services to this group of students. They frequently remain undetected and can be difficult to identify, but they are also one of the greatest at-risk groups. Their concern for their abusing or dependent parent can severely interfere with their functioning in school.

Starting the Group

Starting a concerned persons group can be done by organizing the student body into small groups, again perhaps through homerooms. The use of a film such as the 1985 film *My Father's Son* (Gerald T. Rogers, F.M.S. Productions, Los Angeles) is highly suggested here. The film should portray to the students what life in a chemically dependent family is like. It should convey the essence of the roles acted out in these families but, more important, some of the emotions and feelings experienced by young people in these homes. The showing of the film should be non-threatening and primarily educational in nature. It is helpful to facilitate a discussion after the film about the availability of the concerned persons group. The approach here is matter-of-fact with no value judgment, so that those students who are having problems in this area will consider joining the group. At this point, it is sometimes helpful to have each student voluntarily complete a questionnaire such as the *Children of Alcoholics Screening Test* (Jones, 1983). (See Appendix F for a copy of the test and scoring procedures.) This questionnaire has been researched and comes with a test manual which may be ordered from the publisher. It can be used to determine the severity of parental drinking problems. It identifies adolescents who could benefit from participation in a concerned persons group. Responses to this questionnaire may also be used, if students choose to share them, as a basis for beginning the concerned persons group. Once a group has begun, a core exists and therefore so does the program. Group members will bring their friends, and word will spread about the group and the support that it is offering these students.

Purpose of the Group

There are two purposes of the concerned persons group. The first is to facilitate a discussion of feelings, bringing them out into the open. The second is to provide education concerning chemical dependency, so that students have a context within which to understand those feelings. Groups should be structured to allow for the educational component, yet flexible and open enough to facilitate discussion of related feelings. These groups tend to be emotionally intense, and facilitators should be experienced and relatively comfortable dealing with such intensity. For many students, it will be the first time that they have talked about what it is like to have grown up and lived with a chemically dependent parent. These students will usually not be able to change the situation in which they are living. They need to learn that there are options and that they have choices in terms of their own roles. In this way, they will begin to develop the basic skills necessary to survive as healthy individuals.

These students will need to learn to be responsible for their own behavior, accepting the understanding that blaming their parents' drinking for their own life problems is not personally helpful or productive. Blame is dead-ended and does not create energy or motivation for personal change. These students can learn that they can in fact move forward by making changes in their lives and experiencing competency. For this reason, these groups are most effective when they are action oriented, encouraging students to make gradual changes in their own lives through their own process of acceptance of responsibility for their lives. An underlying goal for these students is an understanding of family roles and how these roles may have served to limit personal options for them and place them at high risk for the development of their own chemical dependency problems.

Format of the Group

The following represents a suggested format for an in-school concerned persons group. The six sessions are listed only for the purpose of providing structure for the educational aspect of this group. This group is viewed as an open-ended group allowing for students to remain in the group as long as it is helpful to them. Group facilitators may complete the education portion early in the group process during a semester and find themselves returning to a specific section as the needs of the group dictate at any given time. It is important to keep in mind that the educational section of this group provides very new material having an intense emotional impact. Students' readiness to understand this material and integrate it will vary. As a given student's emotional awareness increases, the educational material may take on new meaning and the individual may become more receptive to its impact. It is recommended that this group meet once or twice a week for from one to two hours.

Session One: Progression and the Denial System

The first session discusses both the progression of chemical dependency and the denial system from the perspectives of both the chemically dependent person and the family members. Students should be helped to identify their own role in the family denial and how that role took on new dimensions as the family member's drinking or drug use progressed. It is very important in these discussions to never allow the concerned adolescent to feel blame or responsibility as a result of his/her role. The purpose of this group experience is to reduce blame and create freedom for personal growth.

Session Two: Roles in the Chemically Dependent Family

This session discusses family roles (Wegscheider, 1981; Black, 1982). Students are helped to explore the role or roles that they may have played in their own family along with underlying feelings as a result of this role. Students begin to develop a concept of the strengths and weaknesses of each role. It is here, then, that the student will develop the beginning understanding and appreciation for the ability to choose among the roles.

Session Three: Enabling

Enabling is defined. The group facilitator explores with the group enabling situations in which they have been involved. During this session it is important to normalize enabling and the resulting experiences and to also begin to explore healthier options for both the chemically dependent person and the student. Again, it is critical that this be a non-judgmental session. It will not be helpful for these students to experience guilt as a result of an understanding of enabling. They must understand the role of enabling in the entire disease process. The goal is for students to become aware of options available to respond to parents.

Session Four: Feelings in the Chemically Dependent Family

All students will be experiencing some sort of feeling, whether it be anger, hate, resentment, sadness or loneliness. These feelings should be normalized. The student should know that there is nothing wrong with these feelings and begin to develop hope for feeling other ways. It is helpful to discuss the fact that people frequently feel ashamed and guilty about such feelings and try to hide them and keep them secret rather than accept them and move toward a healthier manner of functioning.

Session Five: Detachment and Self-Care

A discussion of love and detachment is the focus of this session. Students are helped to understand that they are not responsible for their parents' drinking or drug use and that they cannot change it. It is strongly encouraged that students be introduced to Alateen, as this can provide a supportive environment outside the school.

Session Six: Exploration of Personal Use

In this session students discuss their own use of alcohol and other drugs. It is important to give a clear message to these students that they are at high risk for developing chemical dependency themselves. It may be helpful to ask the students to consider their entire family, including grandparents, aunts and uncles, and identify those family members who consistently seem to drink too much or get into trouble with their drinking. Since these students frequently come from families with multigenerational alcoholism, they may begin to experience the seriousness of their risk.

Summary

In summary, we see that student assistance programs can provide the help that is needed to keep schools involved in their primary task: that of teaching students. These programs are organized so that teachers have a course of action to follow when problems emerge and students can receive the help they need. These programs work to identify problems, to assist in the resolution of these problems through referrals, and also to prevent these problems from escalating and interfering with the education which must go on in schools.

CHAPTER SIX

THE FAMILIES OF ADOLESCENTS

It was a fine thing of you not to take me with you to town. If you won't take me with you to Alexandria I won't write you a letter or speak to you or greet you . . . Mother said to Archalaus, 'He upsets me, Take him away!' . . . So send for me. I implore you. If you don't, I won't eat, I won't drink; so there!

An Egyptian boy's letter to his father,
in Greek, on papyrus, 2nd or 3rd cent. A.D.,
Bodleian Library, Oxford University

CONFLICT IS NORMAL

IT IS GENERALLY recognized, and often reluctantly accepted, that conflict between parents and children is, at some time or another, inevitable. Sometimes, this conflict begins at an early age, especially with children with certain temperamental characteristics (Thomas and Chess, 1980). As children reach adolescence, there is frequently (some might say usually) a significant escalation in parent-child conflict. This happens even in families where conflict has previously been minimal, and there are a number of reasons for this.

Parents often find it difficult to make the transition in roles necessary to effectively make decisions as the parent of an adolescent. What worked with the young child no longer works with the adolescent. As the young person begins to develop, and express, a separate identity, accommodation within the family becomes more and more of a strain. Sometimes, this provides the setting for the first major family crisis. Things have moved along relatively smoothly until this point. Expectations have been placed by parents and the child has conformed. But now, with the onset of adolescence, there is a dramatic change as the young person begins to assert more independence and reveals needs more reflective of an adult than of a child. In many families this is an alarming turn of events.

Sometimes, the family strongly resists these changes and attempts are made to recreate the original family structure. When this happens it is common for adolescent symptomatic behavior, often alcohol or drug abuse, to emerge. As adolescents move away from the family as the primary socializing influence on their lives, clashes are predictable and, many would argue, unavoidable.

Contributing to this conflict is the fact that the world view of the adolescent is vastly different than that of the parent. These differences emerge in a number of areas but generally reflect the reality that adolescents do not acknowledge, or experience, the limits that parents know are there. Physically, adolescents are at their peak, taking strength and stamina for granted, while parents may be feeling the cumulative effects of age, old injuries, and possibly disease. The adolescent feels invulnerable. In contrast, the adult knows that there is usually a price to pay for poor judgment. To the adolescent, the future is boundless and the present is of primary importance. Parents, on the other hand, have a much more realistic time perspective, knowing that the future does, indeed, have limits. Finally, adolescents are strongly guided by intense emotionality. This can be overwhelming to parents who value a rational approach and who want to reason with their children as a way of solving problems.

PREPARING TO LEAVE HOME

From the time they are born, children are, in many ways, preparing to leave home. Except in cases of extreme retardation or deprivation, children have a natural desire to explore, reach out and expand possibilities. When parents recognize this, there are usually strong feelings of ambivalence. They feel both protective and proud at the same time. The curiosity and risk taking so apparent in the young child's everyday behavior often engenders fear in parents who know that there are very real dangers to which the child may seem completely oblivious. On the other hand, the child's achievements which result from exploration and experimentation are sources of joy to parents who recognize that the child's emerging independence frees not only the child but the parents themselves.

Parents are continually faced with the dilemma of how much to protect and hold on to their children and how much to risk and let go of them. Erring too much in either direction can have detrimental effects. Overprotected children do not have confidence in their own capabilities, and when they do reach out it is often with trepidation. Ironically, they may be more likely to suffer the very consequences that their parents have tried to shield them from. In contrast, parents who allow too much freedom and not enough support and guidance may not provide the security that their children need. Consequently, these children may be quite fearful, because they feel pushed to do things they are not ready or able to do. The ideal is for parents to reach a balance that provides a secure base (a chance to be dependent) and an opportunity for exploration (a chance to be independent).

Balancing their children's needs for dependence and independence becomes especially important for parents when these children reach adolescence. However it also becomes exceedingly more difficult at this time. The following are some common reactions parents use to reassure themselves:

- Kids want limits. It makes them feel secure.
- Kids want limits. They have to have something to rebel against.
- Give them enough rope, they'll hang themselves.
- They're really just little kids in grown-up bodies.
- Who ever said life was easy?
- A little rebellion is normal.
- Let them stay young. You're an adult a lot longer than you're a kid.
- You play with fire, you get burned; some people have to learn the hard way.
- They have to know who's boss. That's the real world.
- You don't learn to walk without falling down.

Of course, all of these statements have their bit of truth, and when parents are faced with an adolescent with a drug problem they are likely to try to seek simple answers. When it has become clear that a young person is involved with drugs, parents are confronted with a situation demanding on-the-spot decision making. At the same time, they are not likely to assume a posture of calm deliberation and rational problem solving. Parental reaction may vary, from throwing in the towel and temporarily giving up, to threatening to kick the adolescent out of the home, to efforts at exerting stringent control, which may, unfortunately, include physical violence.

Because substance abuse is usually accompanied by other defiant behaviors (Hendin et al., 1981), parents quickly assume they have lost all control and, in many cases, it rationally appears they have. Enforcement of structure and limits often seems impossible, especially when drug abuse is part of the picture. Conflict within the family frequently becomes an everyday occurrence.

For those who work with drug-abusing young people and their families, it is a challenge to deal with this conflict. Questions such as these must be addressed:

- How much of the conflict in the family is a result of normal adolescent rebellion and how much is due to the drug problem?
- What should be addressed first — the drug problem or the family conflict?
- Are they related and, if so, how?
- What factors in the family seem to be influencing the problem?

The following section of this chapter explores the factors and dynamics in families that influence adolescent drug use. (Family Therapy is discussed in detail in Chapter Seven, "Treating the Problem.")

PARENTS AS ROLE MODELS

It is commonly observed by those who work in both inpatient and outpatient treatment programs for adolescents with substance abuse problems that, in the families of these adolescents, there is a disproportionately high percentage of family members, frequently parents, who abuse chemicals. Treadway (1985) estimates that 80 percent of the adolescents who have substance abuse problems have parents who also have substance abuse problems. And, as he mentions, this appears to be the general consensus of those who work in the field. In discussing chemical dependency specifically, Alibrandi (1978) describes a residential treatment program where 50 percent of the chemically dependent adolescents had one or more parents who were also chemically dependent. These observations are supported by the findings of research studies which address the question of parental influence on adolescent drug use.

For most adolescents, parents serve as primary role models for a variety of behaviors, roles, attitudes and beliefs. Of course, adolescents themselves do not usually acknowledge this, and many, in fact, spend time and energy attempting to disprove it. However, there is considerable evidence that adolescents strongly reflect their parents' behavior where alcohol and drug use is concerned. Barnes (1986) researched the question of how much influence parental drinking patterns have on adolescent drinking patterns and found that moderately drinking parents are more likely to have moderately drinking children and that ". . . heavier drinkers in this study as well as alcoholics in other chemical studies are more likely than others to have children who are heavier drinkers or have various alcohol-related problems" (p. 34). They conclude that children learn or imitate both positive and negative parental drinking behaviors as they grow up and that such behaviors become incorporated, through socialization, into the young person's own behavior pattern.

These observations are also supported by the studies of Kandel et al. (1978) who found a strong relationship between parental abuse of alcohol and drugs and adolescent chemical abuse, and by Fawzy et al. (1983) who found moderate to strong relationships between parental use of specific substances, including coffee, cigarettes, beer and wine, hard liquor and marijuana/hashish, and adolescent use of such substances.

Adolescent behavior is also influenced by parental attitudes. Adolescents who perceive their parents as having permissive views about drug use are significantly more likely to use drugs than those adolescents who perceive their parents as holding more conservative views about drug use (McDermott, 1984).

ALCOHOL IS A DRUG, TOO

Many parents do not have the same degree of concern when their adolescent drinks as they do when that same young person uses other drugs. Part of the reason for this is the fact that alcohol is a legal drug (although it is not, of course, legal for adolescents). Also, for most adults it is a familiar drug, since a majority of adults in American society do drink alcoholic beverages (U.S. Dept. HHS, 1983). They consume alcohol in a variety of sociocultural contexts which are very similar to the contexts where their adolescents choose to drink. Alcohol is traditionally used to socialize and celebrate by adults, and these are among the reasons commonly mentioned by adolescents to explain why they drink, as well.

Parents who say "it's only booze" are often shocked to find that adolescent drinking has led to the use of other drugs. This does not happen in every case, and there are adolescents, for example, who experiment with wine or beer and stop there. However, Kandel and Faust (1975) have found that the use of legal drugs usually precedes the use of illegal drugs. In other words, it is more common for a user of illegal drugs to have started with the use of legal drugs than to have begun with the use of an illegal drug. Interestingly, these researchers also found that the combined use of cigarettes and alcohol is the highest indicator of likely entry into the use of illegal drugs.

Also, it has been found that, while the imitation of parental alcohol and drug use previously mentioned tends to be consistent for amount of use, it does not necessarily hold for specific substances used. That is, adolescents may generalize the imitative pattern from amount of legal to amount of illegal drugs. For example, an adolescent who has a heavily drinking parent may not only drink heavily but may also be a heavy user of marijuana. These findings are reported in a number of research studies discussed by Fawzy et al. (1983) who also found that adolescents use a greater variety of drugs than their parents do.

It is important to point out, also, that even if the adolescent does not move beyond the sole use of alcohol, there can be destructive results from that use alone. Adolescents can move to the later stages of abuse and dependency while using only alcohol, and problems within the family can be just as devastating as they are in families where adolescents are involved with what are considered to be the more serious drugs. Kaufman (1985b), in his review of two decades of research, has noted: "When the substance abuser is an adolescent or young adult, the family systems which led to substance abuse, or which are in reaction to it, are quite similar regardless of whether the primary substance of abuse is alcohol or drugs" (p. 908).

FAMILY FACTORS

There are other family related factors that appear to predispose young people to problems with drugs. Among them are poor family communication and no apparent praise for good behavior (Reilly, 1976), lack of acceptance, closeness and warmth (Prendergast, 1974), and parental mental illness, divorce, separation and frequent moves (Gibbs, 1982).

Kandel et al. (1978) propose that the quality of the parent-adolescent relationship is a determining factor in influencing whether or not the young person develops serious drug problems. Initial drug use, according to their developmental stage theory, is explained as a result of social behavior and peer influence. When the adolescent moves on to more serious involvement with drugs, they suggest that the cause is adolescent depression and alienation within the family. Based on this, it would seem that family closeness may serve as a protection against adolescent drug problems. It was found by Brook (1980) that affectionate involved parents are much less likely to have adolescents who use illegal substances. A similar finding is reported by Streit et al. (1974), who found that adolescents who do not use illegal drugs show a consistent perception of love from both parents compared with users of these drugs who, in general, perceive parental hostility. Barnes et al. (1986) found a positive relationship between high parental support/nurturance and low incidence of adolescent alcohol abuse.

The importance of parental nurturance as a key factor in preventing serious adolescent problems has been noted by developmental theorists and is summarized by Bronfenbrenner (1981): "In order to develop normally a child needs the enduring, irrational involvement of one or more adults in care of and joint activity with the child. In short, somebody has to be crazy about the kid." (p. 38).

IMPORTANCE OF BALANCE

Balance in parental decision making appears to be another key factor in preventing adolescent drug problems. In 1986, Barnes conducted a study which revealed a relationship between adolescent alcohol abuse and parental control that is quite interesting. They found that parents who exert moderate control in disciplining their adolescents have a low incidence of alcohol abuse among those adolescents, while for both parents who are highly controlling and those who exert low control, there is a higher incidence of adolescents who abuse alcohol.

This need for balance is also pointed out by Kaufman (1985a), who discusses the parental attitudes which seem to insulate adolescents from drug abuse, and then notes: "However, if any of these attitudes are overdone or excessive, then the converse may be true, and overconcerned attitudes may lead to or perpetuate substance abuse." (p. 248).

A DIFFICULT TRANSITION

In healthy families, parental involvement, while still important in the lives of adolescents, takes a different form than it did when they were young children. It is frequently observed by family therapists that families of adolescents who have problems with drugs are frequently struggling with the transition which is necessary for the adolescent to ultimately leave home (Haley, 1980; Stanton and Todd, 1982). There are a number of reasons for this. One commonly noted reason is marital conflict and/or distance which parents choose not to deal with directly. The adolescent sometimes becomes the focus of parental frustration and the scapegoat within the family. Often, one parent (frequently, but not always, the mother) has become emotionally tied to the adolescent in a manner that encourages the adolescent to, partially, take the place of the spouse. This relationship is frequently termed symbiotic. Attardo (1965) compared mothers of adolescent drug addicts to mothers of normal adolescents and found that these mothers and their drug-dependent adolescents had remained strongly emotionally tied to one another, while the mother-child relationship for the normal adolescent had diminished in emotional intensity as the child entered adolescence. Based on their findings, they conclude that this symbiosis is unique to the families of drug-dependent adolescents. Also, a high degree of familial dependence in families of young adult drug addicts was found by Stanton and Todd (1982).

It could be argued that this intrafamilial dependence creates a situation where adolescents must act out through the abuse of drugs and ultimate dependency. It has been suggested that this behavior provides a way for the adolescent to remain dependent in the family at one level, in that parents must remain involved and concerned about the young person. Yet, at another level the adolescent is displaying apparently independent behavior, since his or her abuse of drugs is a behavior neither condoned nor accepted by the parents. This pattern has been described as pseudo-individuation (Stanton and Todd, 1982). The adolescent has not found an appropriate and healthy way to separate from the family and, therefore, resorts to this destructive pattern.

It should be pointed out that this family dynamic could be explained in a different way. As mentioned, when the family focuses on an adolescent who has a drug problem, other family issues are ignored and family activities begin to revolve around the problem. At this point it can be asked, did the family system lead to the substance abuse, or is it a reaction to it?

Family therapists who work with the families of adolescents who have problems with alcohol or drugs consistently face this question. (Family Therapy is discussed in detail in Chapter Seven, "Treating the Problem.")

PARENTAL GUIDELINES

Based on the research, it appears that parents are most likely to avoid serious alcohol or drug problems with their adolescents if they provide the following:

1. Positive role models both in behavior and attitude. That is, they do not abuse drugs or alcohol themselves, nor do they accept such abuse on the part of other people (especially their adolescents).
2. Clear, firmly enforced rules. They outline expectations and limits for their children and they consistently follow through with appropriate consequences when these are not met. They know that this shows the love and concern that young people need (see Appendix H).
3. Involvement in the adolescent's life. They spend time and energy on their children when things are going well. That is, they attend school functions, do things with their children, ask questions, and generally give approval and encouragement. This communicates interest and support and provides a positive context for confrontation which may be necessary later when things may not go well.
4. Separation of issues. They strive to settle their marital issues between themselves and their spouses. They do not involve their children in conflicts within the marriage. They do not let one child's problems take most of their time and energy away from other children. They are direct in dealing with these issues and this is clearly communicated.

risk for continuing alcohol or drug use beyond experimentation (Macdonald, 1984). For this reason, prevention programs should also emphasize activities which enhance building children's self-esteem. In addition, these programs can teach children of parents who are alcoholic or chemically dependent about the risks they face growing up in such a family. Prevention programs can also teach these children about the signs and symptoms of the progression toward chemical dependency which they might identify in themselves should they choose to use alcohol or drugs.

Prevention efforts can also include parent groups. In these groups, parents can be educated about the effect they can have on the attitudes of their children. Adolescents who perceive their parents as having permissive views about drug use are significantly more likely to use drugs than those who perceive their parents as holding conservative views about drug use (McDermott, 1984). Through a prevention program, parents can be informed about the effect their views have on their children's choices and they can be assisted in developing appropriate views.

Intervention

Intervention, here, is defined as a response to any alcohol or drug use by adolescents or talk about using drugs and alcohol among adolescents.

It is critical that adolescents, from experimentation on, receive the message that alcohol or drug use is not acceptable. Parents and other involved adults can intervene effectively if they do not ignore any drinking or drug-taking experience on the part of adolescents. The goal is to recognize and confront the use and provide negative consequences for it. If alcohol or drug use is overlooked, this is giving unspoken approval to it. Consequences that are consistently enforced as soon as there is any sign of use communicate a clear message: Alcohol and drug use will not be tolerated. The adolescent is then making a decision to drink or use drugs with the knowledge that such use may result in a loss of privileges or some other negative consequence.

If an adolescent persists in using alcohol or drugs despite continued consequences, another level of intervention may be required. The adults in an adolescent's life may need to come together in some sort of organized fashion to confront the adolescent with the results of his or her behavior. This type of process can be a very powerful motivator. Along with some pressure (the use of ultimatums), the intervention can provide the impetus for the adolescent to accept that drugs or alcohol are creating some serious problems for him or her. This acceptance is the basis for subsequent change.

Treatment

An intervention usually results in some form of treatment and, at the very least, one last chance for the adolescents to prove that they can in fact put themselves back in control. The abusing or chemically dependent adolescent is at high risk of failing to do this. Treatment occurs at varying levels of intensity and is most often indicated for the categories of misuse, abuse and dependency. The following discussion summarizes forms of treatment, addresses the least restrictive first, and progresses to the most intensive form of treatment.

Outpatient Family Therapy Treatment

Outpatient family therapy can be effective, both in assessing and treating adolescents who show the early signs and symptoms of social use and misuse of alcohol and drugs. Adolescent drug or alcohol use can frequently be viewed as a symptom of a dysfunction within the family (see Chapter Six). For this reason, family therapy is often an appropriate means of assessment and treatment.

In family therapy, the family is assisted in resolving the dysfunctional patterns within the family. If the symptoms of use and misuse then subside, it can be assumed that further treatment is not needed for the adolescent.

In cases where the adolescent is chemically dependent, family therapy is included as an adjunct to a well-structured primary treatment program. (This is discussed in detail later in this chapter.)

Outpatient Primary Treatment

If the adolescent's alcohol or drug use is not arrested or, in fact, increases, and if early signs of abuse are evident, an outpatient primary treatment (OPT) program is indicated. The OPT includes family therapy as a component but moves beyond the family system and focuses also on the adolescent's alcohol or drug problem. The OPT is usually a structured program which includes group therapy, individual therapy and family therapy. The goal is to develop a drug-free life-style while the adolescent is still living at home and attending school. The OPT program works more effectively for those adolescents who are highly motivated to stop using drugs and alcohol and who at the same time have a healthy and strong support system.

Inpatient Short-Term Treatment

If an adolescent is not progressing in an OPT program, a referral is often made to an inpatient treatment program. Inpatient treatment is the recommended treatment for those adolescents who have progressed to the stages of later abuse or dependency. Research indicates that those adolescents completing an inpatient program are more likely to be abstinent at follow-up than those completing an outpatient program (Moberg, 1985).

An inpatient program is a 24-hour-a-day program. The course of treatment can range from two weeks to eight weeks. The inpatient program is typically housed in a hospital setting. However, a number of facilities are developing inpatient programs in residential facilities which adapt the inpatient treatment program to a more home-like and non-medical environment.

The intensity of the inpatient program provides for total immersion in therapy and education about drugs and alcohol and their effects on adolescent lives. This type of program allows the adolescent to experience success at being drug or alcohol free by providing the external controls that the abusing and chemically dependent adolescent cannot provide for themselves. Every aspect of such a program is geared to address the various areas of an adolescent's life affected by drugs and alcohol. For many adolescents, involvement in this type of program is a cathartic and rejuvenating experience and can serve to develop a commitment to a life without drugs or alcohol.

A major goal of an inpatient program is the encouragement of subsequent involvement in a continuing outpatient treatment program. A continuing treatment program addresses many needs unique to the adolescent (such as grief counseling, suicide prevention/intervention and sexuality issues) in addition to the needs specifically related to the problems with alcohol and drugs. The continuing treatment program is designed to help maintain motivation when the initial excitement about being drug or alcohol free begins to subside.

Long-Term Treatment

For some adolescents, the dysfunction in their lives has progressed to such a serious stage that a return to their home and community is unrealistic. For many of these adolescents, a premature return to their home can bring failure. This failure serves to reinforce an already negative sense of self for the adolescent who has already had numerous failures. The long-term treatment program provides ongoing structure so that treatment for the drug or alcohol problems can continue. The long-term program not only provides therapy but facilitates the habilitation of the adolescent. Through this program, the adolescent develops the age-appropriate skills either lost to drug and alcohol use or never developed as a result of the use. The adolescent successfully completing a long-term program is strongly committed to remaining free of drugs or alcohol and to leading a productive life.

Genetic Influences: The Role in Treatment

There is considerable evidence to conclude that there may be a genetic predisposition to alcoholism (Schuckit et al., 1972). Also, it has been noted by Donald Macdonald, a physician and author of *Drugs, Drinking and Adolescents* (1984), that, while there is presently little documented evidence that such a predisposition is true for other chemicals, based on his experience, he believes that such evidence will be found by further research studies.

What does this mean for those who work with young people who have substance abuse problems?

A discussion of the genetic influence in chemical dependence and its role in a treatment program warrants a warning. Chemical dependence is complex. Adolescents do not become dependent simply because they are children of alcoholics. Chemical dependency is not something that simply happens to them, like many physical diseases. Adolescents are not chemically dependent after one use. They must choose to abuse chemicals first. Therefore, it is critical, when integrating the issue of genetic influence into a treatment program, that this not be used as an excuse, and that it be done in such a way that adolescents be allowed to assume full responsibility for dependency. Through the recognition of their participation in the situation, adolescents become empowered to change and grow.

This issue of genetic predisposition has varying implications for treatment, depending on the stage of drug use that the adolescent is in. For example, in addressing primary prevention (prevention occurring prior to any use) and the stages of experimentation, education concerning the vulnerability of adolescents in alcoholic or drug-abusing homes to serious problems with chemical dependency would prove most effective.

This focuses on helping adolescents understand that they are not like young people who come from non-alcoholic homes. It helps them recognize that they are at high risk for progressing to more serious stages of chemical abuse because of the genetic predisposition.

For the adolescent who is misusing and abusing alcohol or drugs, a thorough explanation of the high risks associated with their own substance use, because of their genetic predisposition, could provide the necessary impetus or motivation to halt or decrease their use of alcohol or drugs. For chemically dependent adolescents, an understanding of their own predisposition to chemical dependency may facilitate their ability to accept that their alcohol or drug use has become out of control.

A Dangerous Attitude: Alternative Highs are the Answer

The following question is often asked: "If young people are so motivated by feeling high, then why not help them achieve their highs in alternative and natural ways?" There are some very good reasons to seriously question this approach as the answer to the adolescent drug and alcohol abuse problem. This approach promotes the attitude that we need to feel good all the time. The assumption behind this thinking is that as long as young people are busy and experiencing non-drug-induced highs, they won't be tempted to use drugs and alcohol. There is some truth in this, but there is also danger. The danger lies in teaching young people that life should be one constant pursuit of good feelings when, in fact, quality of life is made up of a range of feelings and emotions. Young people must be taught to deal with, confront and accept the pain and discomfort as well as the pleasant emotions. Most of us experience failure as well as success, rejection as well as love, loss as well as gain, and boredom as well as excitement. Only through experience with the full range of emotions can young people come to feel comfortable with them. If they are encouraged to do something about the less enjoyable feelings, they are given the message that these feelings are bad and must be avoided.

It is important for adolescents to learn that life is not one "high" experience after another. Acceptance of this is a critical element of maturity. Frequently, adolescents describe life as boring. When asked to define what boring means, it often becomes clear that they mean that their life lacks excitement. Young people tend to view things in polarities, and they have difficulty seeing that there are states between boredom and excitement. They need to learn to accept that a lack of excitement does not necessarily mean that something is missing. Encouraging them to seek alternative "highs" when they stop using drugs, or continually attempting to provide such experiences for them, is not beneficial.

This is not to say that involvement in enjoyable leisure time activities is not a positive goal. We believe that young people who are productive and who are experiencing positive reinforcement through any number of activities are less likely to turn to alcohol and drugs. Through these activities they will develop both a positive self-concept and the skills necessary to tolerate a range of emotions and experiences and therefore be less likely to turn to drugs and alcohol to deal with life. The reduction in risk then lies in the skill the young person develops, not in the avoidance of unpleasant feelings. There is a danger in promoting the avoidance of unpleasant feelings. To support participation in activities for the sole purpose of achieving a high is a dangerous approach. It can encourage the idea that the only goal is the high achieved or the avoidance of some sort of unpleasant feeling, rather than the gratification of involvement, participation, and achievement.

Goals and Methods of Treatment

It is a common misconception that the primary goal of treatment programs designed for adolescents with alcohol or drug problems is to get the young person to stop using the substances that have been causing the problem. While it is true that abstinence is an important treatment goal and is, in fact, a necessary condition for further treatment, other factors must also be considered. Underlying issues which are related to the alcohol or drug problem need to be addressed by treatment programs in order to ensure that adolescents embrace and maintain a drug-free life-style.

Responsibility as a Treatment Issue

First, it is extremely important that adolescents accept responsibility for the problems that their use of alcohol or drugs has caused in their lives. Acknowledgment by adolescents of the relationship between their use of chemicals and the problems present in their lives is an essential element in the treatment process.

Adolescents need to recognize that their lives have become out of control, because their alcohol or drug use has become unmanageable. This is an important first step, and until this takes place, further work in the counseling session will need to be postponed. For some adolescents, achieving this recognition can take a long time. Some adolescents require numerous attempts at treatment before they are psychologically secure enough to accomplish this.

Getting adolescents to accept the fact that the problems that are present in their lives are a consequence of their alcohol or drug use is challenging work. First, the problems must be documented. (These may include problems such as family conflict, legal difficulties and unacceptable school behavior or achievement.) Then the young person is confronted about this and is supported in a process aimed toward the acceptance that such a relationship does, indeed, exist. This acceptance lays the groundwork for the move to the more positive aspects of the treatment process. That is, once adolescents have accepted the relationship between their behavior and their problems, they can also consider the possibility of a relationship between their behavior and potential success.

Confrontation in the Therapeutic Program

The unique aspects of adolescent psychosocial development should be understood and incorporated into clinical practice. While many of the dynamics of drug abuse and dependency are similar in both adults and adolescents, the design of their treatment programs should be different.

The more intense active confrontation often present in adult treatment programs may be too threatening, and an anti-therapeutic practice, for young people. This is because adolescents are still forming a personal identity and they may not have the ego strength to withstand such severe confrontation. The sort of attacking strategies often used in adult treatment programs are not appropriate with adolescents whose identities are more vulnerable.

With young people, direct confrontation of self-destructive drug abuse is most helpful when it takes place in the context of a supportive environment and when it focuses on behavior rather than on personal attributes. For example, it is more helpful to point out the specific negative consequences of alcohol or drug abuse, such as poor school achievement or legal difficulties, than to call the adolescent an "irresponsible drunk."

Individuals who are psychologically assaulted feel a loss of dignity and their sense of independence is threatened. This can be devastating for an adolescent in treatment. It is possible for those who work with young people to confront them in a way that maintains the integrity of the adolescent and that is a worthwhile goal in therapy. After all, it is this integrity that allows an adolescent to decide that they are worthwhile and therefore deserve a better life.

Group Therapy

The purpose of group therapy is to provide an opportunity for adolescents to use their interaction in the peer group in constructive and appropriate ways. They can receive feedback from others in the group and, as a result, they can begin to develop greater awareness of their unique identity in relation to other group members. In group therapy, group members confront one another with regard to the self-defeating aspects of drug use and push for individuals to take sole responsibility for their alcohol or drug abuse and to make a commitment to change. While the role of the therapist is important in the group therapy process, the peer group is the central focus in group therapy for adolescent alcohol and drug abusers.

In group therapy with adolescents who have alcohol or drug problems, it is helpful for group members to act as assistants to the group leader in monitoring, advising and confronting one another. It is not beneficial for group members to act as advocates for one another in ways which defend, or make excuses for, unacceptable behavior or which encourage group members to view themselves as victims. If group members begin to advocate for one another, it is highly likely that they will indirectly enable, or support, the adolescent in continuing with alcohol or drug use. It is important that confrontation and challenge take place at this point, not "rescuing." The adolescent's behavior has been destructive and this needs to be acknowledged and addressed. It is the responsibility of the group therapist to facilitate the process and ensure that group members are helpful to each other. The therapist creates a positive peer environment.

As part of the overall treatment program, group therapy has five primary goals. These goals are listed in sequential order. That is, the preliminary steps must be achieved before the subsequent ones can be addressed. These steps have been described by Raubolt and Bratter (1974):

1. Eliminate overt destructive behavior (drugs, violence, manipulation).
2. Encourage (provoke) expression of current feeling (pain, fear, anger).
3. Operationalize current feelings in responsible productive behavior.

4. Foster the development of confrontation, "responsible concern" (not enabling), and encouragement from group members (caring community).
5. Support independent, creative, self-enhancing thinking and action (art, music, political activism, volunteerism).

We see a continuum here from goals which focus on reorientation and reconstruction of behavior through an emphasis on personal growth and development. There is a similar continuum for the goals of individual therapy, as well. However, in individual therapy, there is more opportunity for work on adolescents' personal issues and their unique life circumstances through a one-on-one relationship.

Individual Therapy

The therapist who meets with the adolescent in individual therapy provides an opportunity for the adolescent to develop a healthy relationship with an adult who often serves in many ways as a surrogate parent to the adolescent. Since it is frequently the case that parents of drug-abusing adolescents are overly permissive (Bratter, 1973; Haley, 1980), it is often necessary for the therapist to set limits and take a firm stand in opposition to drug use. It is important that expectations and consequences be clearly delineated. Boundaries defined by the therapist will generally be tested by the adolescent, and if this testing is viewed as the adolescent's attempt to express a genuine need to know specifically what the limits and boundaries are, the adolescent will come to feel secure by noting the therapist's strong response. This process is essential in the establishing of the therapeutic alliance which is the first stage in treatment and which provides a setting in which the adolescent feels both supported and challenged (Bratter, 1973).

Following the establishment of the therapeutic alliance, during which the adolescent develops an attachment to the individual therapist, a stronger element of confrontation, in the context of support, can emerge. The therapist takes an active, even demanding, position with regard to the adolescent's alcohol or drug use and related destructive behaviors. It is important that the issue of drug use be dealt with directly before other therapeutic issues can be addressed.

Once adolescents have stopped using alcohol or drugs, therapeutic treatment can progress to the stage of reorientation and reconstruction of behavior. It is at this point that the process of challenging adolescents to take on more responsibility for decision making and, thus, develop greater independence takes place. It is acknowledged that adolescents ultimately have freedom of choice and options for self-control, and the therapist now serves the function of facilitating the adolescents' clarification of goals, behaviors and consequences. The purpose is to increase adolescents' awareness of the negative effects of their drug use and to assist them in beginning to consider alternatives.

It is at this point in individual therapy that the adolescents' desire to change is discussed and the adolescents are challenged about the authenticity of their wish to remain drug free.

The final stage of individual therapeutic treatment is the phase of "growth and development." The adolescent takes on still greater independence and the role of therapist becomes one of consultant/advisor. Adolescents are encouraged to specify goals and to continue in a process of self-inquiry and self-reflection. They are supported in their efforts and are praised for planning and taking responsibility.

Adolescents progress at varying rates in therapy. Some adolescents never progress beyond the stage of eliminating drug and alcohol use. While this may not be seen as optimal, it is tolerated, since it is accepted that adolescents progress based on individual factors. Adolescents can achieve a productive life without engaging in the full course of individual therapy.

Ideally, of course, the adolescent would progress through therapy to the stage of growth and development. Emotional and psychological maturity reduce the risk of relapse and may even, in certain exceptional cases, allow a return to non-dysfunctional drinking in adulthood (Karasu and Bellak, 1980).

Treatment in individual therapy is primarily aimed at addressing issues related to the adolescent need for development of a separate identity. The objective of this treatment is to take the adolescent from dependency on a strong adult figure through appropriate expressions of independent decision making with support from this adult figure. During this process, the adult provides an assertive and challenging role model for the adolescent by confronting and encouraging the adolescent to take a less passive approach to goal setting and decision making. The adult also models a commitment to a healthy life-style and demonstrates appropriate interpersonal relationships.

Education

The educational component of an inpatient treatment program consists of two parts. The first is chemical dependency education which involves teaching adolescents information about the effects of alcohol and drugs as well as about the progression of drug use through dependence. This part also includes education about family dynamics in relation to alcohol and drug problems. The overall objective of this part of the program is the facilitation of an understanding of the roles that chemicals play in a person's life.

The second part of the educational component of an adolescent treatment program involves the adolescent's academic education. While formal schooling cannot have a primary role in inpatient recovery programs, it does have its place. An in-house teacher is provided, with a certain portion of the day set aside for academics. The teacher will focus on specialized groups of students. These include those who need tutoring to remain current with school work in their home school, those who are behind and need remedial work, those who are working on their high school equivalency degrees, and those who are no longer enrolled in a school and need academic guidance. Such a diverse grouping of students requires that the teacher be flexible, allowing for the academic needs of each student to be met and at the same time allowing for the ever-changing composition of an inpatient unit.

The educational component should be designed so that it provides a positive learning experience, one in which adolescents experience success. When this happens, there is a greater likelihood that those young people will be motivated to continue their education when they leave the treatment program. It is also hoped that those students who have dropped out may consider returning to school. Making the educational experience a positive one is important, because many of the adolescents who have developed drug problems have had negative school experiences usually involving some failure.

The existence of a school program within the treatment program highlights for adolescents the fact that school is an important responsibility in their lives. Chemical dependency and the need for treatment does not excuse adolescents from school. On the contrary, a quality treatment program reintroduces the responsibilities and structure they have been avoiding through their chemical dependency.

Both inpatient and outpatient treatment programs should maintain a constant liaison with the schools from which their patients/clients come. Schools can provide a wealth of behavioral and performance data to aid in diagnosis and ongoing assessment and evaluation. They can be enlisted in an outpatient program by providing ongoing progress reports. And finally they can enhance discharge planning whether it be from inpatient or outpatient. Additionally, many schools have some form of student assistant program to aid students with drug and alcohol problems. Some of these schools have in-school support groups to aid the recovering adolescent (see Chapter Five).

Activity and Leisure Time Use

Chemically dependent adolescents classically experience a relief once they are drug free. Not too soon after this, they experience a great deal of pressure about what to do with all of their extra free time. In 1979, 30 adolescents were surveyed as to their use of leisure time prior to participating in the inpatient program (unpublished report, DePaul Rehabilitation Hospital). "Partying" (drinking and/or using drugs) was reported by 77 percent of the sample as the major use of leisure time with friends. These adolescents are ill-prepared in terms of ability to use leisure time in such a way as to promote individual growth and an alcohol- and drug-free life-style.

The activity program should augment and integrate with the psychotherapy treatment program. A comprehensive activity program will consist of two tracks; these are (1) adolescent occupational therapy, to focus on life skills, and (2) adolescent leisure time. Activities in the occupational therapy track will assist adolescents in developing an awareness of their own abilities in leading self-fulfilling, independently functioning lives and will deal with such issues as self-concept, decision making and assertiveness. The leisure time activities would include the physical, intellectual, spiritual and social areas and can involve both work and play. Such activities would include sports, games, reading, part-time jobs, church activities, volunteer work, dancing and arts and crafts and camping. These activities result in positive and pleasurable experiences and are generally incompatible with drug and alcohol use. They increase self-esteem and lead to long-term satisfaction and self-fulfillment. In addition, they provide a means to enjoy life and relate to both people and the environment without the use of chemicals.

Alcoholics Anonymous and Narcotics Anonymous

A successful adolescent treatment program integrates the philosophy of self-help into the program through AA (Alcoholics Anonymous) and NA (Narcotics Anonymous). Recovering adolescents can be introduced not only to the groups but to the vital role such a support system will play in their recovery. Young people's AA/NA groups provide them with an appropriate peer group and a forum for support and nurturance consistent with their needs and separate from their parents. The AA/NA steps provide a program for living one's life, along with a group with which to identify. This can be very helpful for most young people who are fledgling independents. Knowing they must begin to lead separate lives but not having the skills to be independent, adolescents continually search for their own separate philosophy and value system. The AA/NA program provides a new philosophy that is a healthy presciption for life. Many chemically dependent adolescents enjoy adult AA/NA meetings which become a place of introduction for alternative adult role models. Involvement in AA/NA can provide a beneficial adjunct to treatment programs.

Family Therapy

Including the family in the treatment of drug problems has taken place on a large scale. In a national survey of family therapy and drug abuse, Coleman and Davis (1978) found that of 2,012 agencies involved in the treatment of drug problems, 93 percent included some type of family therapy in the program they provided. In addition, since the term "family therapy" is, in fact, a very general one, the researchers used this national survey to determine which theoretical approaches to family therapy were being reflected in these treatment programs. They found that the ratings of eminent practitioners indicated the following levels of influence, beginning with most influential: Virginia Satir, Jay Haley, Salvador Minuchin, Nathan Ackerman, Don Jackson, Carl Whitaker, Murray Bowen. Since the predominant theoretical influence among these leaders is general systems theory rather than behavioral learning or psychodynamic, it is not surprising that the term family therapy has increasingly begun to be used as a term to describe what actually is systemic family therapy in current discussions of family treatment programs, especially those treating drug problems.

Goals for Family Therapy With Adolescents. The following is a summary of the general goals of family therapy for adolescents. Different therapists may place more emphasis on certain goals than others do, and each may choose to describe goals differently, with some expressing goals much more specifically than others do. Here, goals are described in language reflective of a systems orientation, since this orientation is the most widely used by family therapists in alcohol and drug treatment programs.

1. Parents have taken a position of authority in the family hierarchy without being too rigid or too lax, a position of flexible, consistent control.

2. Adolescents are moving toward independence but with signs of age-appropriate dependence still present.

3. Family members communicate clearly and are involved with one another but are neither enmeshed (overinvolved) nor disengaged (underinvolved).

4. Adolescents behave as peers, with siblings taking neither a parent or child role in relation to them.

5. The family has the resources to survive without the "need" for a chemically abusive or dependent member, and the family shows signs that it will be able to effectively function as children grow up and leave home.

Achievement of these goals means that the family must successfully traverse a difficult developmental passage, and this is a developmental passage for all members of the family even though the adolescent is the more visible carrier of the banner.

Getting Parents Involved. Professionals who work with young people know that family therapy can be helpful, and this is supported by research (Stanton, 1979). However, it can sometimes be difficult to convince parents of this and it is important to handle this issue with care. Frequently, parents of drug-abusing adolescents are reluctant to participate in family therapy and resent any implication that they may have any role in the problem. Their initial reaction to the recommendation that all members attend family therapy sessions is often, "We're not the ones with the problem. Do something about this kid!"

To successfully involve parents at this point, it is important to avoid directly contradicting their view of the situation. The goal of family therapy is to enlist the family as an ally to the treatment process (Haber, 1983). Arguing with them about the need for family therapy is likely to set the groundwork for a power struggle which dooms the therapy at the outset. The idea is to set a tone of cooperation and problem sharing in addressing the problem while providing acceptable and desirable reasons for family involvement. Some possibilities are:

1. "Family therapy can help family members live in greater peace." This can be a powerful motivator, since families with drug-abusing young people are often chaotic, full of conflict and, at times, violent. This rationale blames no one in particular (although each family member certainly has his or her own opinion about who is to blame) and identifies a goal — a calmer, more controlled home — that most family members and the therapist can share.

2. "Family therapy can help improve communication in the family."

Again, this reasoning does not place blame but, rather, identifies an area where people usually need some help. In fact, in the initial interviews which take place when the adolescent is brought in for treatment, parents often identify a breakdown in communication as a major problem.

3. "It is important that parents be informed of their child's progress in treatment and family therapy provides a way for this to take place firsthand." Most parents respond quite positively to this suggestion, primarily because it reinforces their position of authority and respects their right to be informed about the adolescent's treatment program. It can be quite threatening to parents to have their children involved in individual and/or group therapy and the inclusion of family therapy as part of the program helps reduce that threat.

4. "Family therapy can help families prevent similar problems with other children in the family." When parents recognize that one of their children has a drug problem, especially if it is the oldest child, it is natural for them to be concerned about other children in the family. They may have resigned themselves to expecting the same sorts of problems as unavoidable in the future. If they can be helped to see family therapy as a possible way to break a dysfunctional pattern and thereby protect other children in the family, they are much more likely to want to be involved.

Parental Abstinence in Treatment. Some programs providing treatment for adolescents who have drug or alcohol problems require a commitment to abstinence on the part of all family members, including parents, while the family is in treatment. This serves two purposes. First, it allows the therapist to further assess the possibility of problems with alcohol or drug use in the parents. Adolescents are not the only ones who minimize their use, and frequently parents do not accurately report the extent of their use in the initial interview. Reluctance to agree to a contract of abstinence or inability to adhere to such a contract are signs that there may be dependence on the part of a parent.

If parental problems with alcohol or drugs are identified, this can be valuable information. However, timing on addressing this issue is of critical importance. Unless there is immediate danger in postponing the confrontation of this concern, it is best to focus on the identified problem, the adolescent. When there has been some relief from the adolescent's substance abuse and related unacceptable behavior, the problems of the parents can be addressed. The therapist can then use cues from the family to decide when and how this is done.

Even if a parent does have a drinking or drug problem, this does not mean that they do not have their child's best interest at heart. Parents are key influences in helping their children get the most from treatment programs. This is true whether the parent is drinking or not. For this reason, it is unwise to intervene too early and risk defensiveness on the part of the parent, which could then jeopardize the treatment program for the child.

The second reason for requesting a contract of abstinence is the belief that parents are important role models for their children. This request reinforces that assumption and sets the groundwork for further exploration of other ways in which parents set examples for their children. An agreement to abstain is also a statement of support for the adolescent on the part of the parents and this is an important message to the young person.

Family therapy is a critical component of an adolescent treatment program. Because of this, keeping parents involved is extremely important. This takes a skilled family therapist in cases where parents also have alcohol or drug problems.

Types of Family Therapy. The following discussion will clarify differences in six family therapy approaches using categories suggested by Madanes (1981). These are the psychodynamic, behavioral, experiential, extended family systems, structural and strategic. The last four categories would be considered to be more systemic in orientation than the first two. Examples of how these theoretical approaches would be implemented in dealing with families of drug-abusing adolescents are included as well as a case example.

Family therapy based on psychodynamic theory emphasizes a person's past experiences in order to explain his or her present behaviors or symptoms (Ackerman, 1966; Boszormenyi-Nagy and Spark, 1973; Framo, 1970; Napier and Whitaker, 1978). These experiences are explained and interpreted, with a goal being greater awareness, for the individual, of the relationships between these past and present behaviors. This approach emphasizes the appropriate expression of emotion, and, even though sessions include other family members, the focus is on the individual who is the identified patient. The other family members play ancillary roles in assisting in the clarification of issues so that greater personal insight and understanding may occur for that patient.

When an approach based on psychodynamic theory is used with adolescent drug abusers, much time is spent on gathering a family history with emphasis on identifying specific traumatic events which may have resulted in the repression of certain thoughts and emotions. The assumption is that when these issues have been worked through and resolved, the need for the abuse of drugs by the adolescent will have been eliminated because avenues for healthy expression have been opened.

The behavioral school in family therapy (Hawkins et al., 1966; Patterson, 1971; Stuart, 1969) bases interventions on learning theory. As with the psychodynamic approaches, the focus is on the identified patient. However, the methodology of the behavioral approach is quite different than that of the psychodynamic, as are the goals. While the psychodynamic approach emphasizes the past, the behavioral approach places primary importance on the present and specific symptoms. Family members are used in the therapeutic process to provide reinforcement for the identified patient in a systematic plan of treatment involving step-by-step implementation toward desired goals. Clearly specified and measurable changes in behavior are of primary emphasis, with little regard given to personal motivation or emotion.

In contrast to the approach described in dealing with adolescent drug abusers with therapy reflecting psychodynamic assumptions, the approach based on behavioral principles is focused on altering the drug-using behavior. Family members are encouraged to participate in monitoring as well as reinforcing behavior, and success in therapy is measured by the diminishment of drug use and ultimately the elimination of the drug-abusing behavior.

Strict behavioral therapists are not usually interested in stages of abuse or concepts like dependency. Observed behavior is the focus. Family therapists who use the behavioral approach are in the minority of family therapists (Madanes, 1981). However, it is important to note that many non-behavioral therapeutic interventions, particularly those described as structural, could be interpreted through behavioral theory. For example, structural interventions which involve having parents take charge through setting clear limits and consequences are often similar, if not identical, to behavioral approaches. The methods are the same, but as Foley (1979) has stated: "Some family therapists use techniques adapted from behavioral modification. It should be noted, however, that in general, family therapists conceptualize these procedures differently" (p. 480). Thus, the behaviorally oriented therapist may describe an intervention in terms of changing behavior to alleviate the presenting problem, while a structurally oriented therapist would describe a restructuring of the family hierarchy, even though both may be using an identical intervention. This has also been noted by Fishman et al. (1982) in their article on treating adolescent drug abusers.

The experiential school, like the psychodynamic approach, emphasizes the expression of emotion and interpretations (Satir, 1972). However, the present rather than the past is emphasized and clear communication in the present is encouraged. The use of this communication is central in dealing with problems in family relationships, and the assumption is that confrontation and clarification will provide for personal growth for family members and, thus, solution of problems. Therefore, a practitioner using this approach to deal with a drug-abusing adolescent would not be as concerned with the drug-abusing behavior itself as with its implications for the family and for the individual's development within, and in relation to, the family. It is assumed that providing opportunities to deal with this issue directly in family therapy sessions will provide alleviation of difficulties associated with the drug problem.

Extended family systems as an approach to family therapy (Bowen, 1978) emphasize the repeating patterns involved in family issues that are replicated from generation to generation. It is assumed that one must make changes in dealing with one's extended family or family of origin if one is to change that pattern with one's present family. The methodology employed in this approach involves rational, analytical processes and directives, and expression of emotion in sessions is not encouraged as it is in the psychodynamic and experiential schools. It would be important to a therapist dealing with a drug-abusing adolescent and using this approach to examine family patterns of drug use and the functions that such use served in the families of the parents. Involvement of members of the extended family in therapy would be considered to be of paramount importance in breaking the chain.

The two approaches categorized under communication by Madanes (1981) are the structural and the strategic approaches. Both of these approaches are based on general systems theory (Jackson, 1968) with differences in areas of focus. The structural approach emphasizes the hierarchical organization of the family roles in the family, and the various communication structures and subsystem boundaries present within the family (Minuchin, 1974). The strategic approach also focuses on the organizational structure but places more emphasis on sequences and patterns in communication and how they relate to the identified symptom. The structural approach views the presenting problem in the context of the family's development and tends to be more growth oriented than the strategic approach, in that there is less focusing on specific symptoms and more on personal growth (Madanes, 1981). In structural family therapy, interventions are planned so that communication patterns in the family reflect the restructuring desired on the part of the therapist in a variety of settings, including the therapy session itself.

In the case of a drug-abusing adolescent, a structural therapist would first examine the effect of the behavior on the family structure, and the family structure on the behavior, and would ask such questions as, "How does this behavior keep the parents from taking their appropriate hierarchical position?" and "Who is aligned with the adolescent?" The therapist would then identify aspects of the family structure reflected in the maintenance of the behavior, and would plan interventions aimed at remedying the situation.

The strategic approach to family therapy places primary importance on the unique family configuration. As Madanes has stated: "The therapist sets clear goals, which always include solving the presenting problem. The emphasis is not on a method to be applied to all cases but on designing a strategy for each specific problem. Since the therapy focuses on the social context of human dilemmas, the therapist's task is to design an intervention in the client's social situation." (p. 19). Thus, interventions with families of adolescent drug abusers would be individually tailored to the specific family situation.

Through a variety of interventions, often involving the use of metaphor, double bind, reframing and paradox, the therapist seeks to introduce greater complexity and more alternatives to the family in order to prevent the repetition of sequences and change the patterns which originally defined the problem. Because therapeutic interventions are individually tailored, creativity on the part of the strategic therapist is necessary.

In dealing with drug abusers and their families, a combination of the strategic and structural approaches to family therapy has been proposed as the most effective and beneficial by M. Duncan Stanton and Thomas C. Todd in *The Family Therapy of Drug Abuse and Addiction* (1982), and in fact, as reported, these systematic approaches are those most commonly used in drug treatment programs. This success in treatment is attributed to the direct intervention that this approach allows in addressing issues such as detoxification and setbacks.

These researchers also suggest an adjustment when the identified patient is an adolescent. "With families of typical adolescent drug abusers, the structural-strategic mix is somewhat different, with a greater emphasis on structural techniques" (p. 120).

One reason this shift in emphasis is recommended is the primary difference which is present in dealing with families of young adult drug abusers and families of adolescent drug abusers. This difference centers around the issue of separation from the family. With the young adult abuser, this individuation is often a primary goal of therapy (Haley, 1980; Stanton and Todd, 1982). Dependence on the family is seen as an obstacle to be overcome. In contrast, the adolescent drug abuser is necessarily still involved with his or her family, and the adolescent's parents are legally responsible for him or her, and, while work toward separation may be incorporated in the therapeutic process, separation itself is not generally an immediate goal. Therefore, the family hierarchy takes on greater importance, and interventions based on restructuring within the family are seen as appropriate. Because of the significant differences in the life stages of the young adult and the adolescent, the goals of family therapy focus on different issues.

Case Example. The following case illustrates how approaches to family therapy can be integrated:

The identified patient is a 13-year-old male named Rob. He was seen in family therapy while he was a patient in the inpatient adolescent program at a drug and alcohol rehabilitation hospital and following his transfer to the outpatient program. He has been admitted with a diagnosis of cannabis (marijuana) dependency.

Rob's parents had been divorced when Rob was four years of age. His father had been awarded custody of Rob because of Rob's mother's expressed intention to return to nursing school to complete her degree. She requested that the courts place Rob in the primary care of his father until she finished school and would then take over primary responsibility. The judge refused this, granting full custody to Rob's father, and citing the fact that his mother had approximately two years of schooling left. Following the divorce, Rob maintained contact with his mother, seeing her every other weekend. She subsequently remarried and had two daughters by this marriage.

At the time of Rob's admission, he had developed severe problems, both academically and behaviorally, in addition to his problem of drug dependence, as is frequently the case. Initially, both of Rob's parents, Ken and Gail, and his stepfather, Jim, and Rob were included in family sessions. This decision was made because of the continued involvement, on the parts of both parents, in Rob's life.

It was immediately apparent that communication between Rob's parents took place largely through him and that he had begun to take advantage of this situation, often misrepresenting communication and distorting information he was asked to relay. He managed to manipulate situations so that his parents became involved in power plays regarding control of him, and this struggle had escalated, with Rob playing his parents off against one another to a greater and greater degree.

When the family entered therapy, the situation had deteriorated to the point that Rob's mother would suggest that Rob come and live with her whenever he complained about his father. In addition, Rob's father would interrogate Rob after his visits with his mother and would often call her to complain about Rob's treatment at her house.

The following observations were made:

1. Rob's behavior, including his drug use, created conflict but also brought his parents together.
2. The authority structure was not clearly defined in this family.
3. Rob's father never psychologically divorced his wife.

During the first few sessions, things became more tense. The hostility between Rob's father and stepfather became so great that there were threats of physical violence and Rob had begun to use drugs again. At this time, in planning future sessions, a consultation team suggested the following interventions:

1. Make the observation to the family that in many ways Ken seemed to still be "married" to Gail. (This was suggested because of the triangulation which took place in which Rob was used by Ken to gain closer contact with Gail.)
2. Indicate that Rob seemed to be trying to get his parents back together and that this was not going to happen.
3. Request family sessions which included Rob and Ken only, in order to establish a family hierarchy in this subsystem, with Ken in charge.

There were strong reactions to these interventions. Ken reacted to the suggestion that he was still "married" to Gail by asking "How?" It was pointed out that he still called her after Rob's visits and that he did not seem to have accepted the reality that Gail's home was her domain. It appeared that these observations were inconsistent with Ken's view of himself and, subsequent to this, he stopped the calls and Gail's response was predictably positive. In response, she was highly cooperative in placing Ken back in authority and in ceasing to sabotage his efforts to take control where Rob was concerned. Haley and Madanes (1982) have commented on this dynamic of reciprocity in facilitating problem resolution and, in fact, encourage therapists to implement strategies that encourage this.

Once the parents began cooperating on these issues, they also agreed to stop communicating through Rob, and both told him that under no circumstances would they be getting back together.

Rob and Ken continued in family therapy, with Gail and Jim coming in for checkup sessions every few weeks. After six months, the situation remained stable. Ken was setting clear limits for Rob and following through with appropriate consequences. He no longer interfered with Rob's visits with Gail. Gail no longer attempted to sabotage his authority and was, in fact, supportive of it. Rob had been drug free (as documented through urine screens) for the entire time and was actively involved in the outpatient treatment program.

The interventions used with his family were a combination of structural and strategic approaches. Redefining the family structure in an appropriate and workable way (a structural intervention) in conjunction with the introduction of the element of reciprocity (a strategic intervention) helped establish a context where Rob could remain free of drugs.

Characteristics of an Effective Counselor of Adolescents With Alcohol and Drug Problems

Flexibility

Counselors who work with adolescents are most effective when they can rid themselves of rigid views about how young people should dress, speak and think. Skilled counselors can tolerate a broad range of behaviors and are not intimidated by attempts at non-conformity, or even what others may see as bizarre behavior. They recognize these are signs that adolescents are seeking to establish their own identities and not as personal threats to themselves. Those who work well with young people are not easily shocked, even when it may appear that the intent of the young person's behavior is to shock. An adult perspective allows counselors to see adolescent behavior in a broader context, and they are not unnerved by adolescent strivings to be unusual or different. They understand that this is an expected part of growing up.

Personal Warmth and Empathy for Adolescents

It takes a special perspective and a lot of tolerance, patience and perseverance to work effectively with adolescents. It is also important to like them as people and to enjoy working with them. If this is not the case, therapy will be a trying experience and it is highly unlikely that anyone will benefit.

Empathy is frequently mentioned as a core characteristic of an effective counselor. It is traditionally accepted that without empathy, the counselor will make very little progress in working with adolescents. This means that counselors are able to convey the message that they understand and know what it feels like to be an adolescent and to be facing the issues adolescents face.

Skilled counselors can express empathy without placing themselves on a peer level with adolescents. Conveying the message that one understands what it is like to be an adolescent does not mean that one has to act like one. Boundaries between counselor and client should be maintained, and this means that empathy is expressed in a role-appropriate way.

Also, expressing empathy does not imply acceptance of potentially destructive or self-defeating behaviors on the part of the young person. For example, counselors may show that they understand how difficult it is for an adolescent to refrain from using drugs under stressful conditions. This does not mean that they in any way condone such behavior.

Finally, empathy is not sympathy. If the counselor feels sorry for the adolescent and expresses this, this can be counterproductive in the therapeutic process. This sort of attitude fosters dependence and it does not respect the integrity of the adolescent. Being pitied does not make one feel competent or capable. Pity implies that the young person is a victim. This is a message that therapy is intended to change, not perpetuate.

Ability to Set Limits Without Hostility

Counselors of adolescents are most effective when they are able to establish a structure, both within the therapeutic setting itself and in their expectations for the young people they work with. This means these counselors can set clear limits and consequences without being punitive, and that they can directly confront unacceptable behaviors and attitudes without conveying hostility or threat. Skilled counselors provide a setting that is secure and predictable for adolescents. This is especially important in working with young people who have serious problems with alcohol or drugs and whose lives have become out of control. It is very reassuring for these adolescents to work with a counselor who clearly communicates firm and consistent expectations. Adolescents who have problems are a particular challenge to the therapist, and most skilled therapists will admit that they have from time to time become unnerved when faced with a hostile young person who has been coerced into treatment. Therapists tell themselves that the adolescent is "begging for limits underneath the bravado" (which is usually true), but it is still difficult.

In fact, even adolescents who have not been identified as having problems can at times act in ways that are difficult to deal with. Psychologist Joan Newman (1985), in her article, "Adolescents: Why They Are

So Obnoxious," acknowledges this difficulty and outlines some of the developmental reasons for this behavior. However, understanding does not guarantee comfort, and therapists should not only be knowledgeable about adolescent development, they should also be skilled at interactng with adolescents in ways which are helpful.

Sense of Humor

The use of humor can be seen as an aid in the therapeutic process, in that it allows for needed fluctuations in intensity and pacing during sessions. The expression of humor by adolescents does not need to be seen as an avoidance of serious issues. When adolescents choose to joke about certain events, it is far more beneficial for the therapist to view this in a positive light rather than as an attempt to get off the track. When this behavior is seen negatively, this only increases the likelihood that the therapeutic relationship will deteriorate and turn into a power struggle between the counselor and the young person.

In the counseling setting, especially with adolescents, it can be very helpful to be able to look at the absurdity of certain situations and laugh at this together. Humor provides a positive contact between counselor and adolescent and is particularly useful in a context which involves confrontation. With drug-abusing young people, confrontation is an essential element of the counseling process and is necessary. However, this can create a significant amount of tension. A little lighthearted joking or teasing (this does not include sarcasm) can break that tension. It also builds rapport through a shared enjoyable experience. Humor adds lightness to what can be a very serious situation.

The counselor who uses humor does not need to tell jokes or act like a comedian during the session. It is more important that the counselor can appreciate and utilize that which is funny to adolescents and can share that with them. In addition to understanding the need that young people have to use humor in relationships, counselors can greatly enhance their effectiveness by being willing to also laugh at themselves. Acknowledging one's shortcomings and foibles can be very reassuring to insecure young people and can make the counselor seem less intimidating to them.

Special Knowledge and Experiences With Adolescents

In addition to possessing skills in the therapeutic process itself, effective adolescent counselors should be knowledgeable about adolescent development in the context of life span human development. Education in this area is essential. Even though the primary problem the counselors address may be adolescent substance abuse, training in alcohol and drug treatment only is not enough. Understanding the unique characteristics of young people from a developmental perspective is also necessary.

For example, sometime after age 12 an adolescent develops an ability to think abstractly, hypothesizing what might happen and choosing decisions based on the hypotheses (see Chapter Two). An adolescent counselor must be aware of this developmental stage, be able to assess it and choose an appropriate therapeutic approach. Adolescents also begin to develop a sense of morality, of right and wrong, which is interpreted as fair or unfair. As a result, adolescents tend to belabor the "fairness" issue. This can be viewed as argumentative or blaming. The experienced adolescent therapist recognizes this as an adolescent trait and tolerates it with appropriate guidance.

In terms of experience, it is recommended that counselors who specialize in working with adolescents participate in an internship or field work program of at least two years' duration. Supervision during this time will help the trainee recognize and resolve many of the issues that emerge as one works with young people.

Experience definitely helps counselors become more confident and competent in working with adolescents. However, there are advantages to being new to the field. Beginning counselors usually have a high level of motivation, enthusiasm and energy. These counselors have not developed familiar habits and patterns and, therefore, demonstrate creativity and inspiration in the treatment process. This is something that experienced therapists must work to maintain.

Also, a counselor who effectively counsels adolescents should operate from a theoretical perspective. This does not mean that the counselor is tied into one particular therapeutic approach but, rather, that that person has a rationale for therapeutic interventions. In other words, if one were to ask the counselor at any point in a counseling session why a certain question was asked or why a particular confrontation was made, that counselor could explain this behavior within a broader theoretical context. The counselor should have some sense of direction and of how to achieve specific goals, in both the short-term and long-term views of therapy.

Without a theoretical perspective, the counselor risks becoming overinvolved in the treatment of the adolescent. It becomes easy to view the adolescent as a victim. The danger to the therapist is the assumption that they alone can make life better for the adolescent. A theoretical framework helps keep both the adolescent's and the counselor's responsibility for change in perspective.

No matter what the school of therapy, respect for the integrity of the adolescent should be an ethical and professional assumption. This does not mean that a counselor may not be authoritative, confrontive and/or directive at times. It does mean that he or she should not ever be abusive or demeaning. It is normal and expected for young people to feel uncomfortable, confused, even disoriented and angry in therapy sessions. When this happens, the experienced therapist does not take these feelings as personal threats but, rather, recognizes that the expression of these feelings is often a positive sign and is frequently the precursor to change.

Knowledge of Implications of Drug Use

Counselors who work with adolescents who have alcohol and drug problems should have some basic knowledge of specific drugs, their categories, and their effects (Appendices I–O). However, it is even more important that they understand the psychological implications and dynamics associated with drug use, abuse and dependence. They should be familiar with the role that drug use plays in the developmental process of the adolescent (see Chapter Two).

Focusing on the adolescent's particular drug of choice during counseling sessions is not usually helpful. The nature of the relationship that an adolescent has formed with a chemical, whether that chemical be alcohol, marijuana, valium or any other, is the important element. This relationship is essentially the same, regardless of what the specific drug is. This is the topic that needs to be addressed in the therapeutic setting.

It is helpful for counselors to be aware of the drugs currently being used by adolescents and the terms that young people are using to describe them. Being up-to-date on the language that is presently being used adds credibility to the counselor in the eyes of the adolescent and helps the counselor understand what young people are talking about when they discuss their drug use. It is not necessary, however, for the counselor to be a pharmacological expert.

Should people who counsel adolescents with alcohol and drug problems be recovering people, themselves? Those who work in this field of alcohol and drug abuse have varying opinions on this. Those who express those opinions range from those who say that counselors in the field must be recovering to those who say this makes no difference whatsoever.

We believe that, while it is not a prerequisite that counselors be recovering people themselves, there are some advantages to the counselor having had this experience, particularly at certain points in treatment. For example, in the early stages of treatment where young people are struggling with the issue of acceptance of the problem, it can be helpful if they are confronted by a person who has been through a similar experience. This person usually carries more credibility at this point than a person who has not.

However, this issue is not as important in the later stages of therapy and, even in the early stages, it is not absolutely essential that the counselor be a recovering person. There are a lot of effective counselors who work with adolescents who have alcohol and drug problems who have not had such problems themselves.

It is also important to point out that having had such problems, and having had treatment for those problems, does not automatically qualify someone to counsel others. These people also need the same sorts of training that others receive in order to work in the field.

Confidence in One's Self

Effective counselors of adolescents convey a sense of self-confidence and inner strength. They have a clearly defined personal identity and they communicate this directly. Their high self-esteem is evident in the ways in which they present themselves and interact with others.

It is important that counselors of adolescents have resolved, for the most part, the developmental issues of adolescence. These include separation from the family of origin and the establishment of a separate identity. Self-sufficient counselors have come to terms with past conflicts with parents and no longer carry hostility about old issues. They have reached a point where they accept their parents and recognize both their strengths and weaknesses.

Effective counselors have come to terms with their own sense of sexual identity. They project security about this and they can articulate their own values and beliefs about this. They do not try to impose these views on others but are supportive of adolescents who may be struggling with this.

Counselors who have not generally resolved their own adolescent developmental issues are often not beneficial to the adolescents they work with. This is because they may use the young person almost as a surrogate, to work out those issues. For example, a counselor who still has a lot of resentment toward his parents, because he believes his parents were too controlling with him, will have difficulty being helpful to an adolescent who is struggling with a similar situation. The counselor may tend to perpetuate the young person's view of him or herself as a victim.

Skilled counselors do not base their success in counseling on whether or not the adolescents they work with stay chemically free. They know that this measure is only one aspect of the process, and they do not judge themselves as successes or failures based on this. Relapses and setbacks are predictable parts to a treatment program and provide opportunities for learning and change. Secure counselors recognize this and do not see each step of the process as a personal reflection on their abilities. They also recognize the limitations of their impact on the lives of the adolescents they work with. They know that this is relatively minimal in the context of overall adolescent development. For example, when one is working with a 16-year-old, chemically dependent young person, there is bound to be regression along with progression. This is a part of the process of maturation, is recognized and planned for, and is not seen as a therapeutic failure.

Evaluating the Success of Treatment

How does one determine if a treatment program has been successful? Clearly, abstinence from the use of chemicals is a major indicator of success. However, that, in and of itself, is not enough. Other signs are also important because they are predictors of longer-term success. If adolescents stop using alcohol or drugs but show no other changes in behavior, there is little likelihood that they will be able to sustain abstinence.

What are the other signs of success? One important indicator is the adolescent's behavior, which should reflect a sense of greater personal responsibility. This may be demonstrated in the home, the school, or in the treatment program itself. This means that the adolescent takes the initiative in these settings and does not blame others for failures or mistakes. The young person acknowledges the relationship between his or her efforts and environmental responses.

Another positive indicator of success in treatment is that adolescents have found constructive ways to use their time. There should be some type of educational or vocational involvement, possibly a part-time job, in addition to other outside interests which may include sports or hobbies.

Recovering adolescents who have stopped spending time with drug-using friends, and who have found a healthier peer group, have a much better chance of continued success in staying drug-free than those who do not. During adolescence, peers are a powerful influence (see Chapter Four). If adolescents go through a treatment program but then return to drug-using peer groups, it will be extremely difficult for them to maintain their abstinence, as well as their new attitudes and behaviors.

Success in treatment is also reflected in the family setting. Adolescents who have been through treatment programs and who have benefitted from that treatment will show signs of taking responsibility at home. They will cooperate more and will more often take the initiative in helping with household tasks. If they are older adolescents, they may begin the process of leaving home in a planned and logical manner. They will not create a situation or a crisis which forces them to leave home.

Recovering adolescents should have an improved ability to co-exist with other family members. This does not mean that home life is continually harmonious. That would be an unrealistic goal, because some conflict is inevitable in any family. What is important is the way in which that conflict is addressed. Willingness to participate in conflict resolution, negotiation, and problem solving is a positive sign that reflects the adolescent's growing maturity. The young person has learned to deal with differences of opinion in constructive ways that do not escalate the problem but, rather, address and solve it.

Adolescents who have successfully completed treatment also show more empathy for other family members. They are less egocentric and more tolerant of other people. They are more accepting of other family members' shortcomings and they are less defensive about their own.

Many parents expect that once their adolescent has been through a treatment program, this young person will be completely open and self-revealing about everything. While honesty and openness are signs of health, with adolescents it is unrealistic to expect complete disclosure. Because of their developmental stage, it is appropriate for young people to have some privacy. The need to have a sense of their own separateness within the family and the desire to keep some things to themselves is not a negative sign.

Because of the need to eventually separate from the family, adolescents who have been through treatment may still want to be alone, may still dress or wear their hair in non-conforming ways, and may still show signs of moodiness or immaturity at times. Success in treatment does not mean a complete changeover in the adolescent. Indicators of success must be seen as steps in a process made up of positive moments combined with much that is left over from the past. Acceptance of this is critical. Parents who expect a completely different young person to return home after completing treatment will be disappointed. They will need to learn to appreciate the smaller signs of success.

The successful treatment of adolescent drug and alcohol problems in a multifaceted process. Not only must the adolescent's stage of use be determined and addressed, but many aspects of the adolescent's life must be taken into account also. "From a treatment standpoint, it does not matter much which came first — the drugs, the dysfunctional adolescent, or the dysfunctional family. All must be attended to if recovery rates are to be good." (Macdonald, 1984, p. 46).

Effective treatment programs consider the many influences on an adolescent's life and intervene in ways which promote the development of healthy, self-confident and independent young people.

APPENDICES

A. School Checklist
B. Program Organization
C. Philosophy on Student Alcohol and Other Drug Abuse
D. Policy on Student Alcohol and Other Drug Abuse
E. Questionnaire for Suspected Adolescent Alcohol/Drug Problems
F. Children of Alcoholics Screening Test (C.A.S.T.)
G. Alcohol and Drug Use History
H. Guidelines for Parents of Adolescents
I. Information About Commonly Used Drugs
J. Alcohol
K. Marijuana
L. Cocaine
M. Opiates
N. Sedative-Hypnotics
O. Hallucinogens
P. Resource List — Adolescent Chemical Dependency

APPENDIX A

SCHOOL CHECKLIST

Student Name _____

School _____

A thorough assessment of a student's alcohol and drug use includes input and impressions from the school where there is the opportunity to observe the student and any behavioral/academic changes over time. Your assistance in checking the following behaviors as they apply to the student in school or the classroom would be appreciated. Please fill out this form at your earliest convenience and return in the enclosed envelope.

Academic Performance:

_____ Decline in grades
_____ Academic failure

Classroom Conduct:

_____ Cuts class
_____ Is tardy
_____ Is truant
_____ Shows extreme negativism in attitude
_____ Lacks concentration
_____ Lacks motivation
_____ Is disruptive in class
_____ Cheats on assignments and/or tests
_____ Is involved in fights at school
_____ Is verbally abusive and uses obscene language and gestures
_____ Vandalizes school property
_____ Sleeps or "dozes" in class

Other Unusual Behavior Observed:

_____ Has recently shown erratic mood swings
_____ Has made a change in peer group
_____ Has suddenly become popular
_____ Shows disorientation with time and/or memory
_____ Appears depressed
_____ Seems to be a loner, separate from others
_____ Other students have expressed concern about this student's problem

Disciplinary:

_____ Has had frequent disciplinary referrals
_____ Has been suspended
_____ Has been expelled

Appendix A *(continued)*

Substance Use Behavior:

_____ Has been caught using in school

_____ Has come to school high or intoxicated

_____ Has been caught with alcohol, drugs or paraphernalia in school

_____ Has come to a school activity high or drunk

_____ Has expressed concerns about his/her own drinking or using

Family Patterns:

_____ Family has shown motivation to be involved

_____ Family blames school/other professionals for problems

_____ Family is enabling (protecting) the adolescent

_____ There is suspected substance abuse in the family

_____ Family looks to professionals for support/help

_____ Family is cooperative with school interventions

Other: Brief comments regarding the student's behavior and your impressions are helpful. Please include here:

APPENDIX B

PROGRAM ORGANIZATION

```
┌─────────────────────┐
│   Administrator      │
└─────────────────────┘
          │
          ▼
┌─────────────────────┐
│   Coordinator        │
└─────────────────────┘
          │
          ▼
```

Core Team	Advisory Committee
Support services: Guidance Social Work Psychological Services Teacher School Nurse	◄── AODA Counselor Police Officer Judge/Probation officer Parent Recovering Teen Community Service Agency

          │
          ▼

Services

1. Assessment
   Group
   Individual

2. Support

3. Referral

APPENDIX C

PHILOSOPHY ON STUDENT ALCOHOL AND OTHER DRUG ABUSE

The _____ School District recognizes that the use of alcohol and other drugs, and the problems associated with it, are increasing in our society. The school district recognizes that in many instances a person's misuse or abuse of alcohol and other drugs can lead to the illnesses of alcoholism and other chemical dependencies. At some point an individual's use of alcohol and other drugs may be deemed destructive to him/herself or others, causing problems in his/her daily life.

The _____ School District regards alcohol and other drug abuse or dependency as it does any other behavioral/medical problem. The district's primary purpose is to be helpful, not judgmental or punitive in dealing with these problems.

The _____ School District believes that along *with* parents and other segments of the community, the school has a role to play in helping students to make responsible decisions about the use of alcohol and drugs. Therefore, the _____ School District wishes to cooperate with all segments of the community in assisting those individuals who do develop alcohol and other drug-related problems.

APPENDIX D

POLICY ON STUDENT ALCOHOL
AND OTHER DRUG ABUSE

The _____ School District recognizes that students often need education and assistance because a person significant to them is afflicted with chemical dependency, or because they require support in their own decisions not to use or abuse alcohol and/or other drugs. Since chemical dependency is frequently preceded by the abuse of alcohol and other drugs, the school system wishes to provide education and assistance to any student displaying the signs of such harmful involvement. The _____ School District recognizes that chemical use may evolve into chemical dependency, a serious illness, which can be successfully treated if identified early, if appropriate referral to community agencies is made, and if adequate support is afforded to those who are in the process of recovery.

It should be understood by parents, students and staff that all violations of school rules and regulations of state and federal laws will be vigorously enforced by school officials. The students' rights and responsibilities outlined by the _____ _____ School District will be adhered to as the standard administrative practice regarding student discipline and students' rights.

Thus, the _____ School District establishes a program to provide education, assistance and support for students affected by chemical dependency, or other alcohol and drug abuse-related problems, along the following guidelines.

1. The possession, manufacture, sale, use, delivery, or sale of alcoholic beverages or controlled substances by students in school or at school-sponsored events is expressly forbidden.
   a. FIRST OFFENSE: The student will be suspended from one to three school days. The building administrator *may* hold suspension in abeyance if the student sees the student assistance program counselor/coordinator *and* follows his/her recommendations satisfactorily.
   b. SECOND OFFENSE: The student will be suspended for three school days. The building administrator *may* hold suspension in abeyance if the student sees the student assistance program counselor/coordinator *and* follows his/her recommendations satisfactorily.
   c. THIRD OFFENSE: A recommendation for expulsion will be made to the Board of Education. Expulsion *may* be held in abeyance if the student sees the student assistance program counselor/coordinator *and* follows his/her recommendations satisfactorily.

Adapted from Appendix A of *The Student Assistance Program* by Gary Anderson, published by Wisconsin Department of Health and Social Services, Madison, Wisconsin, 1981.

Appendix D *(continued)*

2. The main responsibility for operating the program will be in the hands of each building principal (or his/her designee), who will interpret the district's policy to students, staff, parents, and the community, *and* a student assistance program counselor/coordinator, who will assess the nature and scope of alcohol and drug problems in students referred and make recommendations for the appropriate form of assistance.

3. An essential feature of the program is that students, along with their families, are encouraged to contact staff persons, the building principal, or the student assistance program counselor/coordinator regarding problems with alcohol and other drugs, with the assurance that such contacts will be handled confidentially.

4. In general, students who refer themselves to the student assistance program counselor/coordinator *and* who are making satisfactory progress in following his/her recommendations are not liable to formal suspension from school, athletics, or extra-curricular activities for violations in number 1 *prior* to self-referral.

5. Students may be referred to the student assistance program counselor/coordinator by school staff, other students, parents, or community agencies (i.e. clergy, law enforcement, etc.). Staff members are expected to refer any student who (a) exhibits a definite and repeated pattern of decline in their school performance, which may be alcohol or drug-related, and/or (b) manifests any signs, symptoms, or indications of a chemical problem.

6. Any student judged by the administrator to be a possible danger to himself or to others may be excluded from school until a professional evaluation is obtained. In cases of extended absense, assignments will be provided or homebound instruction initiated.

7. When a referral is made, the student assistance program counselor/coordinator may consult with the student and contact other staff members in an attempt to assess the nature and scope of the student's problem.

8. On the basis of his/her assessment, the resource person may recommend one or more of the following courses of action:
   a. No reason for immediate concern; no chemical problem;
   b. Referral to other resources;
   c. Continued one-to-one involvement with the student assistance program counselor/coordinator or other pupil service staff;
   d. Continued involvement with the student assistance program counselor/coordinator and group experiences;
   e. Referral for outside evaluation;
   f. Inpatient treatment;
   g. Outpatient treatment;
   h. Involvement in AA, Alanon, Alateen.

9. At all times, it is the prerogative of the student and families to either *accept* referral to the student assistance program counselor/coordinator or to outside

Appendix D *(continued)*

assistance, or to *reject* it. Regardless of whether a student accepts or rejects assistance, it still remains his/her responsibility to maintain satisfactory or acceptable levels of performance and conduct or face such legitimate disciplinary action as may be corrective and warranted.

10. If a student *accepts* referral and/or treatment, that fact will be regarded as it would for any illness, with respect to benefits and privileges. So long as a student is involved with the program and is making satisfactory progress, there is no reason why he/she may not remain in school.

11. No records of a student's participation in the program will become a part of the permanent record. The fact of a student's participation in the program, including conversations he/she may have with staff members, will be held strictly confidential as required by federal confidentiality regulations.

12. The awareness and support of parents for a student affected by alcohol and other drug abuse and chemical dependency is extremely important. However, where students or parents do not wish to cooperate in making needed assistance available, the student's status in school may have to be re-evaluated, taking into account the best interest of the student, the nature of the problem, and the health, safety, welfare, educational opportunity, and rights of other students and staff.

13. It is against school policy for anyone — students or staff — in school, on school grounds, or at school-sponsored activities to be under the influence of alcohol or other mood-altering drugs, except as outlined in number 14.

14. Prescription medications are to be construed as exceptions to this policy when used *by* the individual for whom they were prescribed and *in the manner and amount* prescribed.

15. It shall be the responsibility of each building administrator and/or his/her designee to develop procedures consistent with this policy and to provide the necessary orientation and training and staff persons. The building administrator/designee and the student assistance program counselor/coordinator for each building will periodically evaluate the progress of the program and its effectiveness and make annual reports and recommendations to the district administrator.

APPENDIX E

QUESTIONNAIRE FOR SUSPECTED ADOLESCENT ALCOHOL/DRUG PROBLEMS

Do You Have an Alcohol or Drug Problem? You Decide.

Young people hear a great deal about whether drug or alcohol use creates problems for them. Sometimes, it is helpful to take the time to look at your drinking or drug using. Evaluate your own use of alcohol or drugs with this questionnaire. Circle the answer that best describes your feelings or using practices. If you really want to be objective, ask someone who knows you well to give you some honest feedback about how accurate your answers are.

1. Do you think you have a problem with drugs or alcohol? — No / Somewhat / Yes

2. Do you turn down alcohol/ drugs that are offered to you? — Frequently / Occasionally / Seldom

3. How would you feel about a social occasion without alcohol and/or drugs? — At ease / Uneasy / Unpleasant

4. Do you use alcohol/drugs to the point of getting high or intoxicated? — Rarely / Occasionally / Frequently

5. On social occasions, how much do you drink or use drugs? — Less than most / About the same as most / More than most

6. Are you concerned about your present using pattern? — Never / Sometimes / Often

7. Do you use drugs or alcohol before or during work or school? — Rarely / Frequently / Routinely

8. Is it important for you to use alcohol/drugs in order to feel at ease? — Not important / Helpful / Important

9. In choosing friends, is it important that they share your interest in drinking or using drugs? — Unimportant / Somewhat important / Necessary

10. Do you sometimes feel a need to drink or use drugs? — Never / Occasionally / Frequently

Appendix E *(continued)*

11.	What would you say is your most important reason for drinking or using drugs at social events?	To be sociable	To have a better time	To feel at ease
12.	In accepting social invitations, do you ever consider whether or not alcohol or drugs will be present?	Never	Sometimes	Frequently
13.	How do you think you would react to an occasion where non-alcoholic beverages were served or drugs would not be allowed?	At ease	Uneasy	Bored
14.	Have you ever found that you could not remember events associated with a drinking or using experience?	Never	Occasionally	Frequently
15.	Have you experienced any change in your grades as the result of drinking or using drugs?	None	Slight impairment	Considerable impairment
16.	How would you feel if your teachers were to ask about your drinking or drug using?	At ease	Uneasy	Defensive
17.	Have you missed school because of your drinking/drug use?	Never	Occasionally	Frequently
18.	How often have you experienced hangovers?	Rarely	Occasionally	Frequently
19.	How do you feel about the effect which alcohol/drugs tend to provide?	OK	Enjoyable	Not easily obtained
20.	Are you using more alcohol/drugs than you did three months ago?	No	A little	A lot
21.	How important is drinking or using a connection with your social relationships?	Unimportant	Helpful	Essential
22.	How would you describe your own drinking or using practices?	Entirely controlled	Doubtful control	Out of control

Appendix E *(continued)*

	Column 1	Column 2	Column 3
23. How would you feel if a close friend asked questions about your drinking or drug using?	Wonder why	Resentful	Angry
24. Have you been arrested or hassled by the police while under the influence or high?	No	1-2 times	Three times or more
25. Have you changed friends because your old friends don't drink or use?	No	Some friends	All friends
26. Are your parents or family members concerned about your drinking or using?	No particular concern	Some concern	Angry and concerned
27. Have you ever moved or changed schools or lived with another relative because of drinking or drug problems?	Never	On occasion	Frequently
28. What would you say most frequently prompts your present drinking or drug using?	Personal choice	Social opportunity	Meddling interference of others
29. Do you ever feel the need to interrupt your present drinking or using in order to regain control?	Never	On occasion	Frequent effort and concern
30. How do you feel about the effect drinking or drug use has upon you?	No particular effect	Uneasy at times	Frequent feelings of fear and uneasiness
Total	_____	_____ x2	_____ x3

Combined total _____

Scoring—Score each question according to the column in which you answered the question.

            Column 1   1 point
            Column 2   2 points
            Column 3   3 points

Results

30-40	It's not likely that you've reached the stage of problem usage.
40-55	You may be headed for serious trouble with your drinking or drug use. Start thinking about making some changes.
55 or above	You should be looking for help *now*.

APPENDIX F

C. A. S. T.

(Children of Alcoholics Screening Test)

Please check the answers below that best describe your feelings, behavior, and experiences related to a parent's alcohol use. Take your time and be as accurate as possible. Answer all 30 questions by checking either "Yes" or "No."

Sex: Male _____ Female _____   **Age:**_____

Yes	No	Questions
____	____	1. Have you ever thought that one of your parents had a drinking problem?
____	____	2. Have you ever lost sleep because of a parent's drinking?
____	____	3. Did you ever encourage one of your parents to quit drinking?
____	____	4. Did you ever feel alone, scared, nervous, angry or frustrated because a parent was not able to stop drinking?
____	____	5. Did you ever argue or fight with a parent when he or she was drinking?
____	____	6. Did you ever threaten to run away from home because of a parent's drinking?
____	____	7. Has a parent ever yelled at or hit you or other family members when drinking?
____	____	8. Have you ever heard your parents fight when one of them was drunk?
____	____	9. Did you ever protect another family member from a parent who was drinking?
____	____	10. Did you ever feel like hiding or emptying a parent's bottle of liquor?
____	____	11. Do many of your thoughts revolve around a problem drinking parent or difficulties that arise because of his or her drinking?
____	____	12. Did you ever wish you parent would stop drinking?
____	____	13. Did you ever feel responsible for and guilty about a parent's drinking?
____	____	14. Did you ever fear that your parents would get divorced due to alcohol misuse?
____	____	15. Have you ever withdrawn from and avoided outside activities and friends because of embarrassment and shame over a parent's drinking problem?
____	____	16. Did you ever feel caught in the middle of an argument or fight between a problem drinking parent and your other parent?
____	____	17. Did you ever feel that you made a parent drink alcohol?
____	____	18. Have you ever felt that a problem drinking parent did not really love you?
____	____	19. Did you ever resent a parent's drinking?

CAMELOT UNLIMITED – 5 North Wabash Avenue
Suite 1409 – Dt 18C – Chicago, Illinois – 60602
Telephone: (312) 938 – 8861

Appendix F *(continued)*

___ ___ 20. Have you ever worried about a parent's health because of his or her alcohol use?

___ ___ 21. Have you ever been blamed for a parent's drinking?

___ ___ 22. Did you ever think your father was an alcoholic?

___ ___ 23. Did you ever wish your home could be more like the homes of your friends who did not have a parent with a drinking problem?

___ ___ 24. Did a parent ever make promises to you that he or she did not keep because of drinking?

___ ___ 25. Did you ever think your mother was an alcoholic?

___ ___ 26. Did you ever wish you could talk to someone who could understand and help the alcohol-related problems in your family?

___ ___ 27. Did you ever fight with your brothers and sisters about a parent's drinking?

___ ___ 28. Did you ever stay away from home to avoid the drinking parent or your other parent's reaction to the drinking?

___ ___ 29. Have you ever felt sick, cried, or had a "knot" in your stomach after worrying about a parent's drinking?

___ ___ 30. Did you ever take over any chores and duties at home that were usually done by a parent before he or she developed a drinking problem?

___ TOTAL NUMBER OF "Yes" ANSWERS

[C1: ___ C2: ___ C3: ___ C4: ___ C5: ___ C6: ___]

(For scoring directions, see below)

Scoring the C.A.S.T.: Add the number of yes responses.

Interpreting the scores:

0-1   Children of Non-alcoholics

These children most likely have non-alcoholic parents. A score of one might suggest problem drinking.

2-5   Children of Problem Drinkers

These children have experienced problems due to at least one parent's drinking behavior. These are children of either problem drinkers or possible alcoholics.

6 or more   Children of Alcoholics

These are more than likely children of alcoholics. Whether or not the parent is early, middle or late stage alcoholic needs to be determined.

APPENDIX G

ALCOHOL AND DRUG USE HISTORY

	Alcohol	Marijuana (Hashish)	Stimulants (Speed)	Depressants (Valium, Downers)	Inhalants (Glue, Paint)	Cocaine (Crack)	Hallucinogens (LSD, PCP, Mescaline)	Other (Mushrooms, Opiates, etc.)
Age of First Use								
Age of First Intoxication								
Age of Weekly Use Pattern								
Age of Daily Use Pattern								
Frequency in Past 30 Days								
Number of Times Per Day								
Last Use								
Longest Period Without Using								
How Much Do You Need Before Passing Out?								

APPENDIX H

GUIDELINES FOR PARENTS
OF ADOLESCENTS

Family Communication:

Family communication is vital:

- Know where to reach each other by phone.
- Be awake (or awakened) when young people come home at night.
- Assure your children that they can telephone you to be picked up whenever needed.
- Get to know your children's friends and their parents.
- Support all school regulations as a family.

Reasonable Hours:

Reasonable hours are necessary for safety and a sense of security.

On school nights:

- All children should be home evenings unless employed or attending school, church or community events. They should be home one-half hour after these events.

On weekends:

- 6th grade and under, home except for school, church, or community events
- 7th and 8th grades, 9:30 – 10:00 P.M.
- 9th and 10th grades, 10:30 – 11:00 P.M.
- 11th grade, 11:30 – 12:00 P.M.
- 12th grade, 12:30 A.M.

Social Life:

As a parent, you are legally responsible for your minor children and their actions.

- Be alert to the signs of drug or alcohol use.
- Be aware that driving after drinking or drug use is a criminal offense.

Parties: As the parent of a party-goer, feel free to contact host parents to:

- verify the occasion
- check on adult supervision
- be sure there will be no alcohol or drugs.
- express concern if party did not meet above standards

Appendix H *(continued)*

As the host parent:

- encourage your children to tell friends that you will expect parental inquiries about the party
- encourage small parties
- ask anyone with drugs or alcohol to leave
- allow no one who leaves to return
- be a visible host/hostess

Unoccupied homes are often the site of parties. Provide for house supervision when you are away.

Malls and Shopping Centers:

- Be sure your children know where to go for assistance if problems occur.
- Encourage reasonable time limits for shopping.
- Be aware of the amount of money your children have to spend and what items are brought home.

Remember: Appropriate and consistent discipline indicates concern and love.

APPENDIX I

INFORMATION ABOUT COMMONLY USED DRUGS

Classification	Drug	Chemical, Trade and Slang Names	How Taken	Effects Sought	Long Term or Heavy Use Symptoms	Intoxication	Withdrawal
Narcotics	Heroin	Diacetyl-morphine; H, Horse, Junk, Smack, Scag, Stuff, Harley, Harry	Injected Sniffed	Euphoria, Prevent withdrawal symptoms	Addiction, Constipation, Loss of appetite, Toxic syndrome, Shortness of breath, Cold and clammy skin, Lowered Blood Pressure, Drowsiness	Euphoria, Mental Clouding, Tranquility, Drowsiness, Constriction of pupils, Central Respiratory Depression which can cause death	Anxiety, Insomnia; Yawning; Sweating; Running nose; Crying; Dilated pupils, Gooseflesh; Tremors; Chills, Loss of appetite, Abdominal & leg cramps, Rise in blood pressure, pulse, respiratory rate, temperature; Nausea; Vomiting; Diarrhea, Dehydration
	Morphine	Morphine Sulphate; White Stuff, M	Injected Sniffed	Euphoria, Prevent withdrawal symptoms, Pain relief	Addiction, Constipation, Loss of appetite, Toxic syndrome		
	Codeine	Methylmorphine; Schoolbag	Swallowed	Euphoria, Prevent withdrawal symptoms, Pain relief	Addiction, Constipation, Loss of appetite, Toxic syndrome		
	Methadone	Dolophine amidone; Dolly	Injected Swallowed	Prevent withdrawal symptoms, Euphoria	Addiction, Constipation, Loss of appetite, Toxic syndrome		
	Demerol Paregoric Dilaudid Darvon Talwin Percodan Percocet		Injected Swallowed	Euphoria, Prevent withdrawal symptoms, Pain relief	Addiction, Constipation, Loss of appetite, Toxic syndrome, Shortness of breath, Cold and clammy skin, Lowered Blood Pressure, Drowsiness		
Hallucinogens	Mescaline	Buttons, Beans, Cactus	Swallowed Sniffed	Insightful experiences, Exhilaration, Distortion of senses	May intensify existing psychological problems	Rise in pulse, body temperature, blood pressure, pupil size; Visual illusions; Perceptual changes; Mood swings; Blurred sensory perceptions: colors heard, noises seen. Time perception distorted; Depersonalization	No physical dependence or withdrawal
	Psilocybin	Magic mushrooms, Mushroom, Los Ninos	Swallowed	Insightful experiences, Exhilaration, Distortion of senses	May intensify existing psychological problems; Dizziness; Lightheadness; Abdominal discomfort; Numbness of tongue, lips; Nausea; Anxiety; Shivering		
	LSD	Lysergic acid diethylamide; Acid, Sugar cubes, Trips, Windowpane, Blotter, Big D	Swallowed Sniffed Injected	Insightful experiences, Exhilaration, Distortion of senses	May intensify existing psychosis; Panic reactions; Flashbacks; Loss of appetite; Dilated pupils; Nausea; Chills; Changes in perception, thought and mood		
Hallucinogens also Stimulant Analgesic Anesthetic	PCP	Phencyclidine; Angel dust, Hog, Horse tranquilizer; Crystal	Swallowed; Sprinkled on cigarettes	Omnipotence, Sense alteration, Euphoria	Flashbacks, Prolonged anxiety. Social withdrawal, Toxic syndrome, Paranoia, Motor incoordination, Slurred speech, Drowsiness, Numbness of extremities, Depression, Full range unknown	Muscular incoordination, Twitching eyeball, Blurred vision, Slurred speech, Exaggerated reflexes, Rigidity of muscles, Seizures, Feelings of dissociation, Perceptual distortions, Auditory or visual hallucinations, Bizarre behavior, Violence, Coma, Death	No physical dependence or withdrawal

Type	Name / Slang	Method of Use	Desired Effects	Short-Term Effects	Long-Term / Dangerous Effects	Withdrawal Symptoms
	Dagga, Kif, Joint, Reefer, Weed, Dope	Snifted	euphoria, Sociability	Alteration in time perception; Rapid heartbeat; Bad trip; Delirium; Drug precipitated psychosis; Flashback; Impairs short term memory, logical thinking and ability to drive a car or perform complete tasks	...long... or sexual damage; Loss of energy; Confused thinking, Impaired memory; Apathy	Nausea, Vomiting
Sedatives	Quaaludes — Methoqualone; Ludes, Soaps, Quacks	Swallowed	Anxiety reduction, Sleep induction	Respiratory depression, Disinhibition, Belligerent, Violent, Slurred Speech, Lack of motor coordination, Drowsiness, Slowed thinking	Addiction with severe withdrawal symptoms, Possible convulsions, Toxic syndrome	Short acting barbiturates (12-16 hrs) or long acting diazepam (valium) 7-10 days — anxiety, restlessness, loss of appetite, nausea, vomiting. Weakness and abdominal cramps; Rapid heart no beat; Low blood pressure; Tremor in upper extremities; Exaggerated reflexes; Insomnia and nightmares; Possibly delirium, convulsions and death
	Barbiturates — Phenobarbital, nembutal, Seconal, Amytal, Luminal, Blue devils, Yellow jackets, Blue heavens, Downers, Barbs, Red devils, Purple hearts, Rainbows, Double trouble, Christmas trees	Swallowed, Injected	Anxiety reduction, Euphoria, Sleep induction		Addiction with severe withdrawal symptoms, Toxic psychosis, Possible convulsions, Shortness of breath, Coma, Paranoia, Irritability, Violence, Mood swings, Shock	
	Tranquilizers — Valium, Librium, Miltown, Equanil, Serax, Ativan, Tranxene, Dalmane	Swallowed	Relaxation, Calmness		Possible addiction with severe withdrawal symptoms, Toxic syndrome, Drowsiness, Confusion	
	Alcohol — Ethanol, Ethyl alcohol, Booze, Juice	Swallowed	Sense alteration, Anxiety reduction, Sociability	Disinhibition, Slurred speech, Lack of coordination, Memory loss, Poor judgment, Alcoholic breath	Cirrhosis, Toxic psychosis, Neurologic damage, Addiction, Loss of Appetite, Vitamin deficiency; Stomach inflammation, Infections, Skin problems, Sexual impotence	
Stimulant	Amphetamines — Benzedrine; Dexedrine; Methedrine Ritalin; Speed, Bennies, Pep pills, Hearts, Wake-ups, Uppers	Swallowed, Injected, Snifted	Alertness, Activeness, Euphoria	Euphoria; Restlessness; Talkativeness; Repetitive stereotyped behavior; Grinding of teeth; Irritability; Tremors; Mood swings; Rapid heart beat; Hypertension; Dilated pupils; Grand mal seizures; Low body temperatures; Paranoid delusions; Hallucinations; Violent behavior; Possible respiratory arrest and death; death possible from convulsions, heart failure or high fever	Loss of appetite, Hallucinations, Delusions, Toxic psychosis, Violent behavior, Chest pain, Abdominal cramps, Paranoid psychosis, Dilation of pupils, Dry mouth, Fever, Sweating, Headache, Blurred vision, Dizziness	Eats too much, Sleeps too much, Depression, Fatigue, Suicide ideation
	Cocaine — Coke, Snow, Flake Toot, Star dust, Happy dust	Snifted, Injected, Swallowed, Smoked (free base)	Euphoria, Excitation, Talkativeness	Rapid heart beat; Hypertension; Tremor; Fever; Difficulty with breathing; Insomnia; Increased REM sleep; Decreased deep sleep; Loss of appetite; Nausea; Vomiting; Agitation; Anxiety; Restlessness, Irritability; Distractibility; Poor concentration; Impaired memory; Impaired judgment; Hallucinations; Impaired judgment, Hallucinosis; Seizures; DT's, possibly convulsions and death	Depression, Convulsions, Attention loss, Hallucinations, Paranoia, Lethargy, Agitation, Mood swings, Reduction in food and sleep, Fatigue, Sexual impotence	Eats too much, Sleeps too much, Depression, Fatigue, Suicide ideation, Irritability
Varied: Stimulant Sedative Hallucinogen	Inhalants Solvents Aerosols	Snifted	Euphoria, Distortion of senses		Toxic syndrome; Brain, kidney, liver, sexual and other tissue damage; Lightheadedness; Nausea; Sneezing; Coughing, Hallucinations	

Written and distributed by DePaul Rehabilitation Hospital, Milwaukee, Wisconsin.

APPENDIX J

ALCOHOL

The drug ethyl alcohol (ethanol) is the main type of alcohol found in alcoholic beverages. It can be manufactured synthetically or produced naturally by fermentation of fruits, vegetables or grains. A 12-ounce bottle of regular beer contains the same amount of alcohol as a drink made with 1.5 ounces of hard liquor (a mixed drink) or a five-ounce glass of wine.

General Effects

Alcohol decreases the activity of parts of the brain and spinal cord. The drinker's blood alcohol level (BAL) depends on the amount consumed, the rate of consumption, the amount and kind of food in the stomach and the drinker's size, build, experience and frame of mind.

In small quantities, alcohol can induce feelings of well-being and relaxation, and seem to act like a stimulant because it lowers inhibitions in social situations. This is due to the depression of brain functions which control mood and emotion. After more alcohol is consumed, depressant effects dominate. Symptoms of intoxication include becoming flushed and dizzy, losing coordination, slurring speech, unsteady walk and a slowing of reflexes. Judgment and restraint may also be affected. Finally, the drinker is likely to stagger, have double vision, numbing of the senses and stupor. Although it is possible to overdose on extremely large doses of alcohol by anesthetizing the brain's control over breathing, this rarely happens because most people pass out before a lethal dose can be taken. The lethal BAL is approximately 0.5 percent.

Combining alcohol with antihistamines (cold, cough or allergy medications), marijuana, tranquilizers, barbiturates or other "sleeping pills" can dangerously intensify the effects of these drugs. The use of alcohol alone *or* in combination with any of the above drugs impairs one's ability to drive an automobile, operate machinery and perform other similar activities.

Drinking heavily over a short period of time may produce a hangover (headache, nausea, shakiness, etc.) beginning eight to 12 hours later. A hangover is the body's response to withdrawal from alcohol.

Following repeated use over a long period of time, alcohol users can suffer appetite loss, vitamin deficiencies, stomach inflammation, infections, skin problems and sexual impotence or disinterest. Some develop damage to the liver and central nervous system, as well as disorders of the heart and blood vessels. In severe cases, there may be confusion and/or loss of memory and blackouts. Memory loss can be permanent. Death rates for heavy drinkers are much higher than for light drinkers or abstainers.

Appendix J *(continued)*

Tolerance and Dependence

Regular use of alcohol induces tolerance, making increased doses necessary to produce the desired effects. When tolerance develops, alcohol-dependent people may drink large amounts, or steadily throughout the day or evening, without appearing to be intoxicated. Because they may continue to work reasonably well, their condition may go unrecognized until severe physical damage develops, or until they are confined to bed or hospitalized for other reasons, and then experience withdrawal symptoms.

Consistently heavy drinkers are likely to become psychologically dependent on alcohol. The drug becomes so central to their thoughts, emotions and activities that it is extremely difficult to stop use. There is also compelling need or craving to keep taking the drug, and it becomes the central focus of the individual's life. Physical dependence occurs later, and is a state in which the body has adapted to the presence of alcohol, and withdrawal symptoms occur if its use is stopped abruptly. Symptoms of addiction and withdrawal can range from blackouts, jitteriness and jumpiness, insomnia, sweating and poor appetite to tremors, convulsions, hallucinations and possibly death. Thus, alcohol addiction and withdrawal can be a life-threatening problem and needs to be treated as such.

Written and distributed by DePaul Rehabilitation Hospital, Milwaukee, Wisconsin.

APPENDIX K

MARIJUANA

Marijuana or Cannabis, and Hashish are obtained from the hemp plant, *Cannabis sativa*. The main ingredient in cannabis, which produces the typical effects of mood and perceptual changes, is called delta-9-THC. To obtain these effects, the drug is usually smoked in a joint (marijuana cigarette) or a pipe.

Effects

The effects of marijuana depend on the amount taken, the user's past drug experience, the circumstances of use, and the user's frame of mind.

The short-term effects occur rapidly after a single dose and disappear within a few hours. The most common short-term effect of marijuana is a feeling of euphoria (high), often leading the user to talk or laugh more than usual. Other short-term effects include an increase in heart and respiratory rate, reddening of the eyes and later a feeling of sleepiness. There may also be a misjudgment of time, so that a few minutes seem like an hour.

Marijuana intoxication impairs short-term memory, logical thinking, and the ability to drive a car or perform other complex tasks. It adversely affects reaction time, depth perception and peripheral vision. At very high doses, THC may have effects similar to LSD and other hallucinogens.

Long-term effects occur after repeated use over a period of time. Because the tar content of THC smoke is so high (at least 50% higher than that of tobacco), many users have chronic bronchitis and other respiratory problems. The risk of lung cancer is three times as high in chronic THC users than in cigarette smokers. In long-term use, the THC level continues to build up in the body and is slowly and continuously released into the bloodstream even when the user isn't smoking or "stoned."

Chronic heavy users may show loss of drive and energy, slow and confused thinking, impaired memory and apathy. This is often referred to as "amotivational syndrome" and seems to disappear gradually after drug use stops.

Some physicians and researchers believe additional problems include chromosome damage, reduced levels of male sex hormone in the body, reduced body defenses against infection, and brain and liver damage, although these findings have not been consistently supported by research.

Tolerance and Dependence

Regular use of marijuana causes moderate tolerance, making increased doses necessary to produce the desired effects. There is also a mild physical

Appendix K *(continued)*

addiction in heavy, chronic users. Research has also found there to be a psychological dependence in marijuana users. This is marked by a craving, because the drug becomes the focus of the user's thoughts, emotions and activities.

Written and distributed by DePaul Rehabilitation Hospital, Milwaukee, Wisconsin.

APPENDIX L

COCAINE

Cocaine is derived from the leaves of a bush growing in the Andes mountains, primarily Peru and Bolivia. Sold on the street, cocaine is often a fine, white crystalline powder known as "coke," "snow" and other nicknames. It is often diluted with similar-appearing substances such as cornstarch, milk-sugar or other adulterants. Now, a new, chemically different form of cocaine is becoming popular. This free-base form of cocaine is called "crack" or "rock."

Cocaine stimulates the nervous system with effects similar to adrenaline, and almost identical to amphetamines. It is also a powerful local anesthetic. Inhaling cocaine is the most common method of use, but it is also injected just under the skin or into a vein. A dangerous and relatively new way of using cocaine, called "free-basing," is becoming widespread. After it has been treated to change its chemical structure, the drug is smoked, usually in a water pipe.

Effects

The effects of cocaine depend on the amount taken, the user's past drug experience, the circumstances in which the drug is taken, and the user's frame of mind.

In low doses, cocaine produces a short-lived sensation of ecstasy or euphoria with increased feelings of energy, alertness and sensory awareness. It also reduces the need for food and sleep. Large doses may intensify the "high," but can also lead to bizarre, erratic, paranoid and sometimes violent behavior. Physical effects include an accelerated heartbeat, faster breathing, rise in body temperature, dilation of the pupils, sweating and paleness.

Individual sensitivity to cocaine or intentional or accidental overdose can cause restlessness, agitation and anxiousness. Physical effects may include hyperactive reflexes, tremors, incoordination and muscular twitching. In severe cases, cocaine can produce pressure or pain in the chest, nausea, blurred vision, fever and convulsions.

Because of its local anesthetic properties, very high doses of cocaine may ultimately cause depression of the central nervous system, possibly respiratory arrest and death. Convulsions, heart failure or very high fever may also cause overdose deaths.

Chronic cocaine users may suffer significant weight loss, sleep deprivation and loss of sexual interest. Male users may become impotent.

Tolerance and Dependence

Chronic cocaine users appear to experience tolerance, the need to take more

Appendix L *(continued)*

of the drug to produce the same effects. It appears that cocaine may also be the most powerful drug of all in producing psychological dependence. This occurs when the drug becomes so central to a user's thoughts, emotions and activities that it is very hard to stop use. It is under debate whether cocaine causes physical dependence, in which the body adapts its functioning to the drug, and withdrawal symptoms occur when use is stopped. But many people do experience depression and lethargy, long but disturbed sleep, strong hunger, emotional mood swings and irritability when stopping use.

Written and distributed by DePaul Rehabilitation Hospital, Milwaukee, Wisconsin.

APPENDIX M

OPIATES

Opiates are drugs derived from the seed pod of the Asian poppy. They include opium, codeine, morphine and their derivatives (such as heroin). There are also manufactured opiates such as meperidine (Demerol) and methadone. These drugs have been used medically and recreationally for centuries.

Appearance

Opium is generally in dark brown chunks or powder. Heroin may appear as a white or brown powder, which is usually dissolved in water for injection. Most heroin contains a high percentage of milk-sugar, quinine or other substances, which dilute (cut) the drug. Pharmaceutical narcotics are available in tablets, capsules, syrups, etc. Opiate solutions are injected just under the skin or intravenously, or are taken orally or sniffed (snorted).

Effects

The effects of opiates depend on the amount taken, the user's past drug experience, the circumstances in which the drug is taken (setting), and the psychological frame of mind of the user (set).

Short-term effects are those which occur rapidly after a single dose and disappear within hours or days. Opiates briefly stimulate the higher centers of the brain, and depress the activity of the central nervous system. Immediately after injection, the user feels a surge of pleasure (rush) which yields to a state of gratification (high) into which very little can intrude. The body feels warm, the limbs feel heavy, and the mouth gets dry. The user may then go "on the nod," an alternatively wakeful and dreamy/sleepy state in which all is forgotten except feeling high.

At very large doses, the user can't be roused, the pupils contract to pinpoints, the skin becomes cold and clammy, and respiratory depression can become so profound as to cause death.

In therapeutic doses for pain relief, the drug's effects last three to four hours. Pain may still be perceived, but the emotional reaction to it is reduced, so that the person doesn't care about the pain and a state of emotional contentment is achieved.

Long-term effects appear following repeated use over a period of time. Chronic opiate users may develop a number of severe medical problems due to unsterile injection techniques. Various types of pneumonia may develop from the respiratory depression.

Appendix M *(continued)*

Tolerance and Dependence

Regular use of opiates leads to tolerance, so the user must increase dosage to achieve the desired effects. Chronic users may become psychologically dependent on opiates. The drug becomes so central to their thoughts, emotions and activities that it is difficult to stop use. Opiate users also become physically dependent. Their bodies have adapted to the drug's presence and withdrawal symptoms occur when its use is stopped.

Written and distributed by DePaul Rehabilitation Hospital, Milwaukee, Wisconsin.

APPENDIX N

SEDATIVE-HYPNOTICS

Sedative-hypnotics are the class of drugs that act as central nervous system depressants, slowing down or decreasing many body functions, including those of the brain. Barbiturates such as Amytal®, Nembutal®, Luminal®, Seconal® and Tuinol® are the most common examples; but Doriden®, Noludar®, Quaalude® and Placidyl® (all non-barbiturates) are also sedative-hypnotics. These drugs are nicknamed "downers" or "barbs," but there are also specific nicknames that describe individual pills or capsules, such as "reds," "yellows," and "rainbows."

Effects

The effects of these drugs depend on the amount taken, the user's past drug experience, the physical environment in which the drug is taken, and the user's frame of mind.

A small dose of sedative-hypnotics relieves anxiety or tension, producing calmness and muscular relaxation. A larger dose taken in a quiet setting usually produces sleep. An equal dose taken in a more stimulating situation (such as a party) may cause a feeling similar to being drunk. The effects include slurred speech, staggering, slowed reactions and the loosening of normal inhibitions or controls.

Doses larger than prescribed may cause unconsciousness. Even larger doses can cause death by putting the brain's control over breathing to sleep. The combination of sedative-hypnotics with other depressants, such as alcohol, tranquilizers, opiates and antihistamines, significantly increases this risk. It is dangerous to operate machinery or drive a car while under the influence of these drugs, because they can impair judgment and motor coordination.

Tolerance and Dependence

Regular use of sedative-hypnotics leads to tolerance, making increased doses necessary for the desired effects. Tolerance to different effects also develops at different rates. As it takes more and more to get "high," the risk of fatal overdose increases because the tolerance to harmful effects doesn't develop as quickly.

Chronic sedative-hypnotic users may develop a compelling need for the drug known as psychological dependence. This exists when the drug becomes so central to the user's thoughts, feelings and actions that it is very hard to stop use. Physical addiction is the body's adaptation to the presence of the drug.

Appendix N *(continued)*

Sedative-hypnotic addiction is one of the most dangerous of all chemical dependencies. Abrupt withdrawal of the drug leads to increased restlessness, anxiety, insomnia and irritability; possibly delerium, convulsions and death. As with alcohol addiction, withdrawal should be medically managed in a medical setting.

Written and distributed by DePaul Rehabilitation Hospital, Milwaukee, Wisconsin.

APPENDIX O

HALLUCINOGENS

Hallucinogens are drugs that cause radical changes in mental state or mood, involving distortions of reality and hallucinations (perceiving things not really there). Hallucinogens such as LSD, DMT, STP (DOM) and TMA are manufactured illegally. Others include mescaline, which can also be produced synthetically, or extracted from the peyote cactus; and psilocybin, which comes from certain mushrooms. Other naturally occurring hallucinogens are found in morning glory seeds, jimson (loco) weed and nutmeg.

General Effects

The effect of hallucinogens depends on the properties and amount of the drug taken, the user's past drug experience, the circumstances, and the user's frame of mind. One usually has alterations of mood and perception (illusions) when taking low doses. Higher doses can produce actual hallucinations. Users may experience different reactions to the same drug taken at different times. Some find the effects stimulating; others find them unpleasant and emotionally disturbing.

Tolerance and Dependence

Regular use of hallucinogens causes an increase in tolerance, so that the user must take more to achieve the desired effects. There is also a cross-tolerance effect, in which users who have a tolerance for one of these drugs won't experience what they want from another either. Chronic abusers become psychologically dependent on hallucinogens. The drugs become the focus of their thoughts, emotions and activities. There is no physical addiction, however, so there is no withdrawal syndrome when use is stopped.

LSD

LSD is a white, odorless crystalline powder nicknamed "acid." It is found in a fungus which grows on rye and other grains, but can also be manufactured. Although it is sometimes sniffed or injected, the most common ways of taking LSD are swallowing it or putting it under the tongue.

LSD's initial effects are usually felt in less than an hour, and the whole experience may last up to 12 hours. Physical effects include an increase in blood pressure and heart rate, and dilated pupils. Muscle weakness, trembling, nausea, chills and hyperventilation may occur, as well as impairment of motor skills and coordination. The user may experience several different moods

Appendix O *(continued)*

simultaneously, or swing rapidly from one mood to another. Hallucinations are common. Hearing and vision may be intensified or merged, and one's sense of time may be altered.

The "flashback," or recurrence of the sensations that occurred during a prior drug experience, is an effect for about 25 percent of users. It is experienced when the user is *not* under the drug's influence, occurring days, weeks, sometimes years after discontinuing use.

Although there are no known deaths directly attributable to an LSD overdose, there are associated suicide attempts, or deaths due to the inability to differentiate the boundaries of one object and another, and of oneself from the environment.

Written and distributed by DePaul Rehabilitation Hospital, Milwaukee, Wisconsin.

APPENDIX P

RESOURCE LIST
ADOLESCENT CHEMICAL DEPENDENCY

I. TO UNDERSTAND ADOLESCENT CHEMICAL DEPENDENCY

ESSENTIALS FOR THE DIAGNOSIS OF CHEMICAL
DEPENDENCY—VOL. I AND II
McAuliffe, Robert M. and McAuliffe, Mary Boesen, 1975
The American Chemical Dependency Society
5001 Olson Memorial Highway
Minneapolis, MN 55422

DRUGS, DRINKING AND ADOLESCENTS
Macdonald, Donald Ian, 1984
Year Book Medical Publishers
35 East Wacker Drive
Chicago, IL 60601

INSIDE THE ADOLESCENT ALCOHOLIC
Krupski, Ann Marie, 1982
Hazeldon
P.O. Box 176
Center City, MN 55012

ALCOHOL AND ADOLESCENT ABUSE
Flanzer, Jerry and Sturkie, Kenley, 1987
Learning Publications, Inc.
P.O. Box 1326
Holmes Beach, FL 33509

STRATEGIES FOR CONTROLLING ADOLESCENT DRUG USE
Polich, Michael; Ellickson, Phyllis; Reuter, Peeler; and Kahan,
James, 1984
Rand
1700 Main Street
P.O. Box 2138
Santa Monica, CA 90406-2138

THE ASSESSMENT AND TREATMENT OF ADOLESCENT
ALCOHOLISM
Hall, Cecil, 1983
Illinois Alcoholism Counselor Certification Board

Appendix P *(continued)*

104 North Fourth Street
Springfield, IL 62701

ALCOHOL & ADOLESCENTS
Bean, Margaret, 1982
Johnston Institute
510 1st Avenue North
Minneapolis, MN 55403-1607

ADOLESCENT SUBSTANCE ABUSE
Edited by Isralowitz, Richard and Singer, Mark, 1983
The Haworth Press
28 East 22 Street
New York, New York 10010

YOUNG ALCOHOLICS
Alibrandi, Tom, 1978
CompCare Publications
2415 Annapolis Lane
Minneapolis, MN 55441

Films: A STORY ABOUT FEELINGS, Johnston Institute
510 1st Avenue North
Minneapolis, MN 55403-1607

SONS AND DAUGHTERS, DRUGS & BOOZE
Gerald T. Rogers
5225 Old Orchard Road, Suite 23
Skokie, IL 60077

II. FOR PARENTS

HOW TO COPE WITH A TEENAGE DRINKER: NEW ALTERNATIVES AND HOPE FOR PARENTS AND FAMILIES
Forrest, Gary G., 1983
Fawcett Crest by Ballentine Books
201 E. 50th Street
New York, New York 10022

FIVE CRIES OF PARENTS: NEW HELP FOR FAMILIES ON THE ISSUES THAT TROUBLE THEM MOST
Strommen, Merton, P. and Strommen, A. Irene, 1985
Harper & Row
10 E. 53rd Street
New York, New York 10022

Appendix P *(continued)*

PARENTS, PEERS AND POT
Manatt, Marsha, 1979
Publications No. (ADM) 82-812
Department of Health and Human Services Prevention Branch
Division of Resource Development
National Institute on Drug Abuse
5600 Fishers Lane
Rockville, MD 20857

PARENTS PEERS AND POT: AN UPDATE
Korcok, Milan, 1982
Health Communications, Inc.
2119-A Hollywood Blvd.
Hollywood, FL 33020

KIDS AND DRUGS: A HANDBOOK FOR PARENTS AND
PROFESSIONALS
Tobias, Joyce, 1986
Panda Press
Annendale, VA 22003

. . . BUT I DIDN'T MAKE ANY NOISE ABOUT IT
Lewis-Steere, Cindy, 1980
CompCare Publications
2415 Annapolis Lane, Suite 140
Minneapolis, MN 55441

NOT MY KID: A PARENTS' GUIDE TO KIDS AND DRUGS
Polson, Beth and Miller, Newton, 1984
Avon Books
The Hearst Corporation
1790 Broadway
New York, New York 10019

STEERING CLEAR: HELPING YOUR CHILD THROUGH THE
HIGH RISK YEARS
Cretcher, Dorothy, 1982
Winston Press
430 Oak Grove
Minneapolis, MN 55403

Film: SONS AND DAUGHTERS, DRUGS & BOOZE
Gerald T. Rogers
5225 Old Orchard Road, Suite 23
Skokie, IL 60077

III. ABOUT CHILDREN OF ALCOHOLICS

IT WILL NEVER HAPPEN TO ME: CHILDREN OF
ALCOHOLICS AS YOUNGSTERS, ADOLESCENTS,
ADULTS, 1982
M.A.C. Printing and Publications
1850 High Street
Denver, CO 80218

CHILDREN OF ALCOHOLICS: A GUIDEBOOK FOR
EDUCATORS, THERAPISTS, AND PARENTS, 1979
Ackerman Learning Publications
P.O. Box 1326
Holmes Beach, FL 33509

REPEAT AFTER ME
Claudia Black, 1985
M.A.C. Printing & Publications
1850 High Street
Denver, CO 80218

Film: MY FATHERS SON, Gerald T. Rogers
5225 Old Orchard Road, Suite 23
Skokie, IL 60077
LOTS OF KIDS LIKE US, Gerald T. Rogers
5225 Old Orchard Road, Suite 23
Skokie, IL 60077

IV. FOR SCHOOLS

ONE STEP: EARLY INTERVENTION STRATEGIES FOR
ADOLESCENT DRUG PROBLEMS, 1986
Muldoon, Joseph A. and Crowley, James F.
Community Intervention
529 South Seventh Street, Suite 570
Minneapolis, MN 55415

THE STUDENT ASSISTANCE PROGRAM: THE WISCONSIN
EXPERIENCE, 1986
Anderson, Gary L.; Krebsbach, Sara; Fredlund, Susan
Wisconsin Department of Health and Social Services
Division of Community Services, Bureau of Community Programs
Office of Alcohol and Drug Abuse
DePaul Training Institute
4143 S. 13th Street
Milwaukee, WI 53221

Appendix P *(continued)*

WHEN CHEMICALS COME TO SCHOOL: THE STUDENT
ASSISTANCE PROGRAM MODEL, 1987
Anderson, Gary L.
Community Recovery Press
P.O. Box 20979
Greenfield, WI 53220

ALLIANCE FOR CHANGE: A PLAN FOR COMMUNITY
ACTION ON ADOLESCENT DRUG ABUSE
Crowley, James, 1984
Community Intervention, Inc.
529 South Seventh Street, Suite 570
Minneapolis, MN 55415

WHAT WORKS, SCHOOLS WITHOUT DRUGS
U.S. Department of Education, 1986
1-800-624-0100

Films: A BETTER TIME, A BETTER PLACE, COMMUNITY
INTERVENTION
529 South Seventh Street, Suite 570
Minneapolis, MN 55415

CHOICES & CONSEQUENCES, Johnston Institute
510 1st Avenue North
Minneapolis, MN 55403-1607

V. FOR ADOLESCENTS

WHY AM I AFRAID TO TELL YOU WHO I AM? INSIGHTS
ON SELF-AWARENESS, PERSONAL GROWTH AND
INTERPERSONAL COMMUNICATION
Powell, John, 1969
Drug Communications
Allen, TX 75002

STEP 1, FOR YOUNG ADULTS, Van Dyke, Della & Nakken, 1986
STEP 2, FOR YOUNG ADULTS, Nakken, June 1986
STEP 3, FOR YOUNG ADULTS, Van Dyke, Della, 1986
STEP 4, FOR YOUNG ADULTS, Bjorklund, Paul, 1986
Hazeldon
P.O. Box 176
Center City, MN 55012-0176

DIFFERENT LIKE ME: A BOOK FOR TEENS WHO WORRY
ABOUT THEIR PARENTS' USE OF ALCOHOL/DRUGS

Appendix P *(continued)*

Leite, Evelyn and Espeland, Pamela, 1987
Johnson Institute
510 1st Avenue North
Minneapolis, MN 55403-1607

VI. ABOUT CONFIDENTIALITY/LEGAL ISSUES

KIDS, DRUGS & THE LAW
Evans, David G., 1985
Hazeldon
P.O. Box 176
Center City, MN 55012-0176

THE COUNSELORS GUIDE TO CONFIDENTIALITY
Weger, Christine and Drehl, Richard, 1984
Program Information Associates
Dept. Box 26300
Honolulu, HI 96825

VII. STATISTICS

DRUG USE AMONG AMERICAN HIGH SCHOOL STUDENTS, COLLEGE STUDENTS AND OTHER YOUNG ADULTS
Johnston, Lloyd D.; O'Malley, Patrick M.; Bachman, Jerald G.
National Institute on Drug Abuse
5600 Fishers Lane
Rockville, MD 20857

REFERENCES

Ackerman, N. (1966). *Treating the troubled family.* New York: Basic Books.

Alibrandi, T. (1978). *Young alcoholics.* Minneapolis, MN: CompCare Publications.

Anderson, G.L. (1981). The student assistance program: An overview. Madison, WI: Department of Health and Social Services, Division of Community Services, Bureau of Alcohol and Other Drug Abuse.

Attardo, N. (1965). Psychodynamic factors in the mother-child relationship in adolescent drug addiction: A comparison of mothers of schizophrenics and mothers of normal adolescent sons. *Psychotherapy and Psychosomatics, 13*(4), 249-255.

Barker, R.G., and Gump, P.V. (1964). *Big school, small school: High school size and student behavior.* Stanford, CA: Stanford University Press.

Barnes, G.M., Farrell, M.P., and Cairns, A. (Feb. 1986). Parental socialization factors and adolescent drinking behaviors. *Journal of Marriage and the Family, 48,* 27-36.

Black, C. (1982). *It will never happen to me.* Denver, CO: M.A.C.

Boszormenyi-Nagy, I., and Spark, G. (1973). *Invisible loyalties.* New York: Harper and Row.

Bowen, M. (1978). *Family therapy in clinical practice.* New York: Aronson.

Bratter, T.E. (1973). Treating alienated unmotivated drug-abusing adolescents. *American Journal of Psychotherapy, 27*(4), 585-598.

Bronfenbrenner, U. (1981). Children and families: 1984? *Society, 18,* 38-42.

Brook, J.S., Gordon, A.S., and Brook, D.W. (1980). Perceived paternal relationships, adolescent personality, and female marijuana use. *Journal of Psychology, 105,* 277-285.

Coleman, S.B., and Davis, D.I. (1978). Family therapy and drug abuse: A national survey. *Family Process, 17,* 21-29.

Coopersmith, S. (1967). *The antecedents of self-esteem.* San Francisco, CA: W.H. Freeman.

Csikszentmihalyi, M. and Larson, R. (1984). *Being adolescent: Conflict and growth in the teenage years.* New York: Basic Books.

Elkind, D. (1967). Egocentrism in adolescents. *Child Development, 38,* 1025-1034.

Fawzy, I.F., Coombs, R.H., and Gerber, B. (1983). Generational continuity in the use of substances: The impact of parental substance use on adolescent substance abuse. *Addictive Behavior, 8,* 109-114.

Fishman, H.C., Stanton, M.D., and Rosman, B.L. (1982). Treating families of adolescent drug abusers. In *The family therapy of drug abuse and addiction*. New York: The Guilford Press.

Foley, V.D. (1979). Family therapy. In R. Corsini (Ed.), *Current psychotherapies*. Itasca, IL: F.E. Peacock Publishers.

Fowler, R.C., Rich, C.L., and Young, D. (1986). San Diego suicide study II: Substance abuse in young cases. *Archives of General Psychiatry, 43,* 962-965.

Framo, J. (1970). Symptoms from a family transaction viewpoint. In A. Ackerman, J. Lieb, and J. Pearce (Eds.), *Family therapy in transition*. Boston: Little, Brown.

Gallup, A.M. (Sept. 1986). The 18th annual Gallup poll of the public's attitudes toward the public schools. *Phi Delta Kappan, 68*(1), 43-59.

Gibbs, J.T. (1982). Psychosocial factors related to substance abuse among delinquent females. *American Journal of Orthopsychiatry, 52*(2), 261-271.

Glynn, T.J. (1981). From family to peer: Transitions of influence among drug using youth. *Journal of Youth and Adolescence, 10*(5), 363-383.

Grande, A., Holloway, W.S., and Evans, C. (Oct. 1986). Dealing with high-risk students: Drug and suicide problems. *PBSA Bulletin*, 18-21.

Gregory, T.W. (1978). *Adolescence in literature*. New York: Longmans.

Haber, R.A. (March 1983). The family dance around drug abuse. *The Personnel and Guidance Journal*, 428-430.

Haire, D.B. (1978). A new look at drug abuse in childbirth. In L.J. Kaslof (Ed.), *Wholistic dimensions in healing: A resource guide*. Garden City, NY: Doubleday and Co., Inc.

Haley, J. (1980). *Leaving home*. New York: McGraw-Hill.

Haley, J., and Madanes, C. (1982). Seminar on structural family therapy. Milwaukee, WI.

Halikas, J.A., Lyttle, M.D., Morse, C.L., and Hoffman, R.G. (Nov./Dec. 1984). Proposed criteria for the diagnosis of alcohol abuse in adolescents. *Comprehensive Psychiatry, 25*(6).

Hawkins, R.P. et al. (1971). Behavior therapy in the home: Amelioration of problem parent-child relations with the parent in a therapeutic role. In J. Haley (Ed.), *Changing families*. New York: Grune & Stratton.

Hendin, H., Pollinzer, A., Ulman, R., and Carr, A.C. (Sept. 1981). Adolescent marijuana abusers and their families. *NIDA Research Monograph, 40,* 17-25.

Huberty, D.J., and Malmquist, J. (Jan.-Feb. 1978). Adolescent chemical dependency. *Perspectives in Psychiatric Care, XVI*.

Hurlock, E.B. (1973). *Adolescent development*. New York: McGraw-Hill Book Company.

Ingersoll, G.M. (1982). *Adolescents*. Lexington, MA: D.C. Heath and Company.

Jackson, D.D. (Ed.), (1968). *Therapy, communication and change*. Palo Alto, CA: Science and Behavior Books.

Jalali, B., Jalali, M., Crocetti, G., and Turner, F. (1981). Adolescents and drug use: Toward a more comprehensive approach. *American Journal of Orthopsychiatry, 51*(1), 120-130.

Johnson, L.D., Bachman, J.G., and O'Malley, P.M. (Feb. 20, 1987). 12th annual survey by the University of Michigan Institute for Social Research. *The University of Michigan News and Information Services News Release*.

Jones, J.W. (1983). The children of alcoholics screening test. In *The children of alcoholics research series, Vol. I.* Chicago, IL: Camelot Unlimited.

Kandel, D.B., and Logan, J.A. (19--). Patterns of drug use from adolescence to young adulthood. I: Periods of risk for initiation, continued use and discontinuation.

Kanel, D.B., and Faust, R. (1975). Sequence and stages in patterns of adolescent drug use. *Archives of General Psychiatry, 32,* 923-932.

Kandel, D.B., Kessler, R.C., and Margulies, R.Z. (1978). Antecedents of adolescent initiation into stages of drug use: A developmental analysis. *Journal of Youth and Adolescence, 7,* 13-40.

Karasu, T.B., and Bellak, L. (1980). *Specialized techniques in individual psychotherapy.* New York: Brunner Mazel.

Kaufman, E. (1985a). Adolescent substance abusers and family therapy. In M.P. Mirkin and S.L. Komar (Eds.), *Handbook of adolescent and family therapy.* New York: Gardner Press.

Kaufman, E. (1985b). Family systems and family therapy of substance abuse: An overview of two decades of research and clinical experience. *The International Journal of Addictions, 20*(6 & 7), 897-916.

Lavenhar, M. et al. (1972). A survey of drug abuse in six suburban New Jersey high schools: The characteristics of drug users and non-users. In S. Einstein and S. Allen (Eds.), *Student drug surveys.* Farmingdale, NY: Baywood Publishing.

Madanes, C. (1981). *Strategic family therapy.* San Francisco: Jossey-Bass Publishers.

Macdonald, D.I. (1984). *Drugs, drinking and adolescents.* Chicago, IL: Year Book Medical Publishers.

McAuliffe, R.M., and McAuliffe, M.B. (1975). *Essentials for the diagnosis of chemical dependency: Vol. 1 and 2.* Minneapolis, MN: The American Chemical Dependency Society.

McCreary-Juhasz, A. (1975). Sexual decision-making: The crux of the adolescent problem. In R.E. Grinder (Ed.), *Studies in adolescence.* New York: Macmillan.

McDermott, D. (Spring, 1984). The relationship of parental drug use and parent attitude concerning adolescent drug use. *Adolescence, XIX*(73).

Minuchin, S. (1974). *Families and family therapy.* Cambridge, MA: Harvard University Press.

Moberg, D.P. (1985). *The social control of deviance: Intervention with adolescent alcohol and other drug users.* Unpublished doctoral dissertation, University of Wisconsin-Madison.

Muldoon, J.A., and Crowley, J.F. (1986). *One step ahead: Early intervention strategies for adolescent drug problems.* Minneapolis, MN: Community Intervention, Inc.

Napier, A.Y., and Whitaker, C.A. (1980). *The family crucible.* New York: Harper and Row.

Newman, J. (Fall, 1985). Adolescents: Why they can be so obnoxious. *Adolescence, XX*(79), 635-644.

Patterson, G.R. (1971). *Families: Applications of social learning to family life.* Champaign, IL: Research Press.

Peele, S. (Dec. 1984). The cultural context of psychological approaches to alcoholism: Can we control the effect of alcohol? *American Psychologist, 39*(12), 1337-1351.

Pizer, H. (1982). *Guide to the new medicine.* New York: William Morrow and Company, Inc.

Prendergast, T.J. (1974). Family characteristics associated with marijuana use among adolescents. *International Journal of the Addictions, 9,* 827-839.

Raubolt, R., and Bratter, T.E. (1974). Games addicts play: Implications for group treatment. *Corrective and Social Psychiatry, 20*(4), 3-10.

Reilly, D.M. (1976). Family factors in the etiology and treatment of youthful drug abuse. *Family Therapy, 2,* 149-171.

Rossman, M.L. (1982). Imagine health! Imagery in medical self-care. Presentation at the Power of Imagination: Uses of Imagery in the Healing Arts Conference, Chicago, Illinois.

Satir, V. (1972). *Peoplemaking.* Palo Alto, CA: Science and Behavior Books.

Schuckit, M.A., Goodwin, D.W., and Windkur, G. (1972). A half-sibling study of alcoholism. *American Journal of Psychiatry, 128,* 1132-1136.

Sheppard, M.A., Wright, D., and Goodstadt, M.S. (Winter, 1985). Peer pressure and drug use: Exploding the myth. *Adolescence, XX*(80), 949-958.

Stanton, M.D. (1979). Family treatment approaches to drug abuse problems: A review. *Family process, 18,* 251-280.

Stanton, M.D., Todd, T.C., Heard, D.B., Kirschner, S., Kleinman, J.I., Morvatt, D.T., Riley, P., Scott, S.M., and Van Deusen, J.M. (1978). Heroin addiction as a family phenomenon: A new conceptual model. *American Journal of Drug and Alcohol Use, 5*(2), 125-150.

Stanton, M.D., and Todd, T.C. (1982). *The family therapy of drug abuse and addiction.* New York: The Guilford Press.

Stephenson, J.N., Moberg, P., Daniels, J., and Robertson, J.F. (Oct. 12, 1984). Treating the intoxicated adolescent: A need for comprehensive services. *JAMA, 252*(14), 1884-1888.

Streit, F., Halstead, D.L., and Pascale, P.J. (1974). Differences among youthful users and nonusers of drugs based on their perceptions of parental behavior. *The International Journal of the Addictions, 9,* 749-755.

Stuart, R.B. (1969). Operant interpersonal treatment for marital discord. *Journal of Consulting and Clinical Psychology, 33,* 675-682.

Thomas, A., and Chess, I. (1980). *The dynamics of psychological development.* New York: Brunner Mazel.

Todd, M.C. (1985). The need for a new health program. In S. Bliss (Ed.), *The new holistic health handbook.* Lexington, MA: The Stephen Greene Press.

Treadway, D.C. (1985). Comprehensive family treatment of substance abuse. Presentation for Clinical Training and Education Associates, San Diego, CA.

U.S. Department of Health and Human Services (1983). Alcohol and health. Fifth special report to the U.S. Congress on Alcohol and Health from the Secretary of Health and Human Services. Washington, D.C.: U.S. Government Printing Office.

Uzgiris, J.C., and Hunt, J. McV. (1975). *Assessment in infancy.* Urbana, IL: University of Illinois Press.

Wegscheider, S. (1981). *Another chance: Hope and health for the alcoholic family.* Palo Alto, CA: Science and Behavior Books.

INDEX

Blotter (*see* LSD)
Blue devils (*see* Barbiturates)
Blue heavens (*see* Barbiturates)
Booze (*see* Alcohol)
Boszormenyi-Nagy, I., 126, 179
Bowen, Murray, 123, 128, 179
Bratter, T.E., 118, 119, 179, 182
Bronfenbrenner, U., 105, 179
Brook, D.W., 179
Brook, J.S., 105, 179
Buttons (*see* Mescaline)

C

Cactus (*see* Mescaline)
Cairns, A., 105, 179
Cannabis sativa (*see* Marijuana)
Carr, A.C., 101, 180
Chemical abuse (*see also* Drugs)
 as meeting needs of kids, 24
 as statement of independence, 25-26
 complexity of problem, 23-24
 role of during adolescent development, 23-
  35 (*see also* Adolescent development)
 to alleviate stress of self-consciousness, 30
 to reduce sexual conflict, 31
Chemical awareness group
 another's story session, 91-92
 as part of assessment, 85-86, 87
 case examples, 86, 87
 closure session, 92
 defenses and denial session, 91
 evaluation session, 92
 for alcohol/drug abusers, 83-84
 format of group, 88
 intervention defined, 85
 organization of, 84
 orientation session, 88-89
 personal assessment session, 90-91
  questionnaire used, 150-152
 personal contract session, 91
 problems beginning group, 85
 progression session, 89-90
  exercise used, 89-90
  questions for, 90
 purpose of, 84
 reassessment and recontracting session, 91
 the family session, 91
Chemical dependency
 abuse versus, 22

adolescents and *see* Student assistance program)
children of chemically dependent parents,
 54-56
 case illustration, 55-56
 meaning of term, 37
 physical signs and symptoms, 43
 program concerns, 4
 resources for understanding, 172-173
 symptoms, 47-53
  blackouts, 49-50
  denial, 51-52
  increased tolerance, 49
  life problems, 52-53
  loss of control, 50-51
  preoccupation, 48-49
  use increasing qualities more frequently,
   52
Chess, I., 99, 182
Christenson, Steve, ix
Christmas trees (*see* Barbiturates)
Cigarettes, trends in prevalence of, tables, 8,
 9, 10
Cocaine
 attitude high school seniors toward use, 7
 effects of, 164
 effects sought, 158, 159
 methods of use, 158, 159
 names used for, 158, 159
 percent high school seniors using, 6-7
 source of, 164
 symptoms
  of intoxication, 158, 159
  of long-term or heavy use, 158, 159
  of withdrawal, 158, 159
 tolerance and dependence, 164-165
 trends in prevalence of, tables, 8, 9, 10
Cognitive powers
 development of abstract thinking, 32-33
 interferences of drugs in thinking process,
  33
 language and the subculture, 33
Coke (*see* Cocaine)
Coleman, S.B., 123, 179
Community center, referral adolescents to
 treatment center by, 39
Competence and adolescents and lack of self-
 confidence, 28
Concerned persons group
 detachment and self-care session, 97